DISCOVERING GOD'S PROMISE

*365 Daily Devotionals to Empower,
Uplift, and Encourage*

Marlon A. Brown

CW00552406

Published by Promise Principles, LLC

Published in Orlando, Florida on December 1,
2023.

www.promiseprinciples.com

Library of Congress Control Number: 2023922024

ISBN: 9798218317256

Contents

Foreword

In 2016, God touched my heart about empowering, uplifting, and encouraging people, so I began sending out daily devotions by text message. What started with just a couple of people eventually grew into a group of hundreds. My goal is to help people on their daily walk in the journey we call "life," so I decided to create this book to enable a larger group of people to feel empowered based on the principles of God's Word. I pray that these devotions become part of your daily routine. There is one for each day of the year, but you don't have to use them in any specific order, and you may find that certain devotions speak to specific challenges in your life.

The Scriptures in these devotionals come from the King James Version (KJV), New Living Translation (NLT), God's Word (GW), Amplified (AMP), and the American Standard Version (ASV) editions of the Holy Bible.

Please feel free to write in your own notes in the margins, or wherever space allows.

Day 1: The Process

Understanding the process starts by faith in the spiritual realm.

Scriptures says:

So do not throw away this confidence; trust in the Lord. Remember the great reward it brings you; patient endurance is what you need now, so that you will continue to do God's will.

Hebrews 10:35-36

You must go through the process. The process is critical to your spiritual development. God does not do quick work, and He does not take away your circumstances or issues overnight. You will have to endure the process because the process is designed to develop you spiritually.

Just hold onto God's unchanging hand. Victory is ours!!! Bible tells us: we can do all things through Christ who gives us strength. Amen!! Amen!!

Day 2: Put God First

Does it seem like no matter how many times you try, it just does not work the way you planned it? For some reason you just cannot seem to get ahead? Put God First!!

You tried your way, and it did not work. You trusted friends and thought they had your back. Every time you turn around, it seems like you are under attack. You have been lied to. You lost your job. Your healing is taking forever. Your bills are due. You trying to figure out which way God is leading you. You have helped others and now you cannot find any help. What do you do? Put God First!!

See, as soon as you wake up in the morning you should be thanking the Lord before anything thing else. Throughout your day you should be thanking the Lord. When it comes to deciding, you should consult with the Lord. Developing a consistent habit of putting God first will allow you to experience all that God has for you. Not your way, His way!! Put God First and watch Him show up and show out in any situation. Amen!! Amen!!

Scriptures says:

But seek ye the Kingdom of God, and His righteousness; and all these things shall be added unto you.

Matthew 6:33

Day 3: Remain In The Lord

Scriptures says:

Remain in me, and I will remain in you. For a branch cannot produce fruit if it is severed from the vine, and you cannot be fruitful unless you remain in me. Yes, I am the vine; you are the branches. Those who remain in me, and I in them, will produce much fruit. For apart from me you can do nothing.

John 15:4-5 NLT

This Scripture is telling us exactly what to do if we Believe what it says. Pray, Stay in God's Word, Meditate on His

Word, and experience peace, comfort and happiness and all God's blessings. If we do not then we will experience all kinds of discomfort, sadness, anxiety, stress, and anger.

My Brothers and Sisters, let us choose to "REMAIN IN GOD." In Jesus name, Amen!! Amen!!

Day 4: Are You Hurting? Please Forgive!

Have You Been Hurt?

It is unlikely that any one of us has made it through life without being hurt by someone, but we only continue letting what they have done hurt us if we do not forgive them.

Ask yourself if you are angry with anyone for anything, and if you are, ask God to help you forgive, forget, and let it go. Please!! Do your best and let it go so you can experience all God's blessings.

Do yourself a favor right now and refuse to remain angry or bitter. God has good things planned for us, and we don't want to miss them by refusing to let go of things in the past. Start fresh with a peaceful heart and be determined to enjoy each day.

Let us pray:

Father God, help us forgive everyone who has hurt us in the past, and if we have hurt anyone, please help them forgive us. In Jesus name, Amen!!!!

4

Day 5: He's An On-Time God

Remember that song by Dottie Peoples? "He's on time God, yes He is. Ooh, on time God yes, He is. He may not come when you want Him, but He will be there when you need Him, He's an on-time God, yes He is."

No matter what we are going through, remember God comes through on time in our victories! Despite the setbacks, holdups, waiting periods, or seasons of perceived stagnation. Trust that God is working everything out for your good, and has positioned you for greatness for His divine purpose and plan.

So when you feel like your dreams will not come to pass, or defeated in many areas of your life, or things appear to not be moving along or forward, trust that God is coming through for you in a timely victory.

Just continue to stay in God's Word, Believe His Word and Trust that He's an on-time God. This way when VICTORY, PROSPERITY, HEALING, FAVOR, and DIVINE PURPOSE show up and show out, then you and others will know: "If it had not been for the LORD on my side!!!!" In Jesus name, Amen!! Amen!!!

Day 6: Don't Blame God

A lot of times we blame God for our lives, problems, struggles, and circumstances, but He is not the blame...

Ok: you may be struggling with your finances. Ask yourself, why/what am I spending my finances on???

Ok: you may be experiencing health related issues. Ask yourself what am I doing/putting into my body???

Ok: you may be experiencing marital issues. Ask yourself why/what happen that got us in this position of distress???

Ok: life may not be going as planned. Ask yourself what choices did I make along the way???

See, God will allow us to do what we want but there are consequences for our actions and choices we make. The bottom line is to make GOD at the CENTER of EVERY AREA of OUR LIVES, and He will guide us through by making Godly choices versus Worldy choices. Amen!!!

Scriptures says:

I am the vine, you are the branches; he who abides in Me and I in him, he bears much fruit, for apart from Me you can do nothing.

John 15:5

Day 7: Let God Be God, You Be You

See, God has done everything for us over 2,000 years ago when He shed His blood on the cross. Now our part is to get in agreement with His Word so we can experience all that He has done.

See, we think we can get God to fix our problems, issues and situations. We Can't!! Have Faith. We Can!!! Believe His Word, Study His Word, and Act on His Word. We Can!!

Truth of the matter is God has done all He's going to do. It is up to us to Believe His Word and do all we can to take hold of what God has made available to each of us. Let God Be God, and we do what we need to do to receive God being God. Amen!!!

Such things were written in the Scriptures long ago to teach us. And the Scriptures give us hope and encouragement as we wait patiently for God's promises to be fulfilled.

Romans 15:4 NLT

Day 8: Wanna Experience The Blessings?

First, we must understand the requirements before Jesus died versus after Jesus died. This is critical ladies and gentlemen to experience the blessings. See, if you are operating under the old Covenant, that is not valid. The new Covenant is valid.

For instance, in Deuteronomy 28:2-3: "If thou shall harken unto the voice of the Lord God, blessed be in the city and blessed shall be in the field." So basically this Scripture is saying we must first obey, then we will be blessed. Meaning if you do good, then God will bless. This was true under the Old Covenant. However, we now live under the New Covenant which is God's Grace.

Grace is undeserved favor, which means we don't earn it, it's is simply a gift from God. All He requires us to do is Believe His Word, and we shall experience His Blessings. In Jesus name, Amen!! Amen!!!

Day 9: Our Help Is From The Lord

Scriptures says:

I look up to the mountains– does my help come from there? My help comes from the Lord, who made heaven and earth!

Psalms 121:1-2 NLT

See, when I cannot seem to get over that hump, I understand my help comes from the Lord! When my down seems up and my up seems down, I understand my help comes from the Lord! When I am stressed and worried, I understand my Help comes from the Lord! When I do not understand why, I understand my help comes from the Lord. When favor is pouring into life, I understand my help comes from the Lord!

No matter what is going on in our lives, we must remember that our help is from the Lord, and He will continue to change, mold, prosper, and guide us into victory through Christ Jesus. Amen!! Amen!!

Day 10: Don't Fake It

Our outward religious activities are important only if they reflect our love for God and others. Be genuine!!

We can always fake our behavior, and we can outwardly fake our love for God. Wondering why things have not gotten better or you just cannot figure it out? Do not fake it!!

If we just go through the motions as if we really love God and others, but our actions say different, and make no real commitment to God, we cannot make progress for long. But if we are motivated by our love for God and other people, our outward behavior will be the natural result of inner devotion!!

See, Being Authentic means always demonstrating love to others regardless of their flaws. Meditating on God's Word day and night, always praising God, and truly resting and trusting God as peace guards your heart. Amen!! Amen!!

Day 11: Fight! Fight! Fight!

Scriptures says:

Fight the good fight for the true faith. Hold tightly to the eternal life to which God has called you, which you have declared so well before many witnesses.

1 Timothy 6:12 NLT

Have you ever thought to yourself and wonder, "when does it stop, when will I see my breakthrough? I am tired of fighting! As soon as I whip one problem, there are a hundred more knocking on my door!"

One thing I can say, we have two choices: to FIGHT, or RETREAT and give in. Retreating is not an option, my brothers and sisters!!!!!!! FIGHT ON!!

Right now, you may be thinking, "if you only knew what I am going through. I am not sure how much fight I have

9

left." That is nothing but the devil. Rebuke him!!!!! Bind that negative spirit!!!! Start calling things that be not as though they were...

When you face the pressure of battle, when stress and trouble come, when you are about to faint, point towards yourself and say, "I'm the righteousness of God in Christ Jesus and I conquer all. No weapon formed against me shall prosper. If God is for me, who can be against me?" Focus your attention on the truth that Jesus is risen from the dead and you are in Him! When He arose, you arose. When He defeated the devil, you defeated the devil. His victory is our victory! In Jesus name, Amen!! Amen!!!

Day 12: What A Mighty God He Is

Scriptures says:

God is our refuge and strength always ready to help in times of trouble.

Psalms 46:1

Even strong young lions sometimes go hungry, but those who trust in the Lord will lack no good thing.

Psalms 34:10

And it's impossible to please God without faith. Anyone who wants to come to Him must believe that God exists and that He rewards those who sincerely seek Him.

Hebrews 11:6

These are just a few Scriptures of GOD'S Word. If we just believe, meditate, and trust GOD'S Word, then we can have and do all that He says we can. We do not have to

10

worry because we know we have VICTORY over our circumstances and challenges!!! Amen!! and Amen!

Day 13: Open Your Eyes To Faith

Are you going to follow the way of the world and fleshy desires? Or will you choose to follow Christ Jesus?

See, those folks who do not have faith cannot SEE past the physical world around them. They are limited by their temporal circumstances, and are blind to what God is really doing. But those who OPEN their spiritual eyes can SEE the spiritual realities which transcend this world.

When our hope is in God's strength and in His faithfulness, we shall find the strength to endure the challenges of life.

However, I will say Faith is never easy. But the more convinced we are of the reality of an all-good, all-powerful God, the more our trust will grow, and the less we will be overwhelmed by doubts and temptations. In Jesus name, Amen!!! Amen!!!

Day 14: Free From Worrying

Scriptures says:

Give your burdens to the Lord, And He will take care of you. He will not permit the godly to slip or fall.

Psalm 55:22

11

Let us pray:

Dear Father, thank you for your strength, comfort and peace. Thank you for allowing me to accept the things I cannot change, to change the things that I can, and the wisdom to know the difference. Help me to live in the present rather than worry about the future. When my mind starts wandering to things that it should not, do something to reel me back to focus on You, Lord. Thank you, Lord, for freeing me from the burden of worry, and increasing my faith in you. This way Lord, I will experience Joy, Peace, and Happiness. In Jesus name, Amen!!!

Day 15: Praise Him In The Middle Of It

Do you feel like your faith is weakening? Is your heart heavy? Are you wondering, "when and how will my situation change?" You may be thinking, "I have just about taken as much as I can take." I encourage you to remember where your help comes from. Do not worry about what you are going through. Instead of worrying, Praise Him in The Middle of It!!!!

See, God knows exactly what you are going through. He has been there all along. He just wants you to trust Him and believe His Word. Just Praise Him in The Middle of It!!!

Scriptures says:

The Lord is my strength and my song; He has given me victory. This is my God, and I will praise Him-my father's God, and I will exalt Him!

Exodus 15:2

Day 16: T-R-U-S-T

Just think about this word: *trust*. It is more powerful than we can Imagine…

T- stands for **trusting** God no matter what the situation or circumstances may look like.

R- stands for **rest,** which mean no worrying about the situation, and letting God know I believe.

U- stands for **understanding** God's way and not ours.

S- stands for **speech**. We must speak it into existence that we will overcome.

T- stands for **thanksgiving**. Thank Him for what He's already done, and what He's getting ready to do. We must always thank God because He is an awesome God, Wonderful Counselor and a Way Maker.

WILL YOU TRUST HIM? Amen!!!!

Day 17: Enjoying Your Life Begins With A Choice

Although we do not have the power to change every unpleasant circumstance in our lives, we do have the power to change our outlook. We can look at life from our innermost being with our hearts filled with positive thoughts and attitudes or we can respond with negative thoughts and attitudes. Your Choice!!!

The bottom line is that we want to be happy and enjoy life. Sadly, we waste most of life with the misconception that joy and enjoyment come from our circumstances, but the truth is they come from our attitude toward each circumstance rather than the circumstance itself.

Nobody enjoys a troubling or painful circumstance, but we need to look at it in a hopeful and faith-filled way, and watch God work.

Scriptures says:

And we know that God causes everything to work together for the good of those who love God and called according to His purpose for them.

Romans 8:28

Day 18: No Need To Worry, Seek Jesus First

A lot of time, we spend too much energy on worrying about Today and Tomorrow. We are concerned about our health, relationships, prosperity, deliverance and etc.... Instead, we should be focusing more on Jesus. He promises to give us a peace that can only come from Him.

Should you be concerned about your health? Yes. Should you make efforts to eat wisely and exercise? Yes. Should you manage your money well? Yes. But to be bound to worry on these things will only prevent you from enjoying your health and blessings.

Seek first His kingdom and His righteousness, and all these things will be added to you.

Matthew 6:33

The problem with worry is that we are seeking the wrong things first and we need to seek God FIRST and His kingdom and everything else will fall into place. In Jesus name, Amen!!! Amen!!

Day 19: Believing The Best

See, the person who is close to God thinks positive and uplifting thoughts about other people as well as about themselves and their own circumstances.

Remember that whatever is in your heart will come out of your mouth carrying creative or destructive power.

I encourage you to send thoughts of love toward other people. Speak words of encouragement. Come alongside others and urge them to press forward in their spiritual life. Speak words that make others feel better and that encourage and strengthen them.

We all have enough problems already. We do not need to add to anymore troubles by tearing someone down. Let us continue, and start believing the best. We are living in obedience to the Word of God when our thoughts, actions, and attitudes line up with what the Word of God says. Amen!! Amen!!

Day 20: Why You Need To Read The Bible

The Bible is no ordinary book. The words within its pages are like medicine to your soul. It has the power to change your life because there is life in the Word!

When you discover the power and truth of God's Word, you will begin to see changes in your life that only this truth can bring. You will also learn how to recognize the lies that the enemy tries to bring against you.

If you are just starting to study the Bible or feel intimidated by it, do not think you have to read it all at once or understand everything right away. Be patient with yourself. The important thing is that you start somewhere and stay determined to learn, meditate and apply.

As we spend time reading and meditating on the Word of God and learn to agree with it above all else, we will be filled with the life and healing power of God.

Let us pray:

God, thank You so much for the life-giving power of Your Word! As I read and study it, teach me what You want me to know and bring Your healing power into my life. Amen!! Amen!!!

Day 21: Don't Grow Weary

God is a merciful God, and He is always ready to help us. God provides comfort and encouragement if we put our trust in Him. We got to trust Him though.

There are times in our spiritual journey where we get tired and weak. Maybe you have been praying and praying and wondering when will my prayers be answered. Got to Believe what you are praying for no matter how long!! We think sometimes that God has forgotten us. He has not!! We may feel completely overwhelmed by our problems and situations and think God is nowhere to be found. Not true!! We must remain confident in the Lord and continue to Trust His Word. His Word will see us through. It will!! Amen! Amen!

Scriptures says:

But I trust in your unfailing love. I will rejoice because you have rescued me. I will sing to the Lord because He is good to me.

Psalm 13:5-6 NLT

Day 22: Developing Trust

Ok, how many times have we allowed trying situations that come our way to frustrate us and get us upset? How many years of our lives have we spent saying, "Oh, I'm believing

God, I'm trusting God," when we are worrying, talking negatively, and trying to figure everything out on our own?

See, a lot of times we think we are trusting God just because we are saying the words, but inside we are anxious, stressed, and worried, and not trusting God at all. Trusting God is more than just words—it is words, attitudes, and actions.

Trust and confidence are built up over a period. Therefore meditating on God's Word is critical. It usually takes some time to overcome a habit of worry, anxiety, or fear. That is why, my Brothers and Sisters, it is so important to "hang in there" with God.

Do not quit and give up. Why? Because you gain experience and spiritual strength as you go through situations. Each time you become a little stronger than you were the last time. Sooner or later, if you do not give up, you will find yourself in a place of complete rest, peace and trust in God. This way you can experience all that God's has for you. In Jesus name, Amen!! Amen!!!

Day 23: Press On!

Maybe you did not get that job promotion you were looking for. Press on! Maybe your marriage or relationship is not working the way you would like. Press on! Maybe your healing is taking longer than expected. Press on! Whatever it is you may be dealing with, I encourage you today to just press on!!

Sometimes things do not work out the way you may have planned them, but it will work out for your good if you just Trust God.

18

Sometimes God's leadership can be most clearly seen in the things that do not work out. Press on when it seems that circumstances are conspiring against you. God's is at work amidst disappointments, cancellations, obstructions, and delay. Now you call it disaster, but one day you may call it GRACE. Amen!!! Amen!!!!

Day 24: The Greatest Blessing

The quickest way to be blessed is to decide to be a blessing to others. When you choose to have a generous heart that reaches out to meet the needs of those around you, God pours His provision into your life.

Something deep in the heart of every believer wants to help others. However, selfishness can make us so aggressive about our own desires that we become oblivious to the needs around us.

With God's help, we can strive in giving to others. If we do so, we will find that God makes sure we have enough to meet our own needs plus plenty to give away.

There is no greater blessing than giving to others in need. In Jesus name, Amen!!! Amen!!!

Day 25: Joy!

Scriptures says:

Weeping may endure for a night but joy cometh in the morning.

Psalm 30:5

Many of us drag around in defeat day after day, month after month, year after year. "I just can't figure it out. I believe the Bible. I believe Jesus has set me free from this sickness. I believe He has set me free from this sin... I believe He has set me free from this lifestyle of lack. But somehow I still can't get the victory." What is the problem, we ask?

The problem is, we are too spiritually weak to receive and comprehend what Jesus has given us: JOY!!!

Scriptures says:

The joy of the Lord is my strength. Joy comes to me!

Nehemiah 8:10

That verse is literally true if you will believe the Word of God. Now, there a difference between *joy* and *happiness*. Happiness comes and goes based upon your situation, but joy is a spiritual force deep within the heart that will last and be there in times of Trials and Tribulations.

Now this Key:

If you are a person of Faith, it does not matter how dark conditions may seem to be right now, you can rest assured a brighter day is on the way. Remember and Apply Gods Word.

Day 26: Things Are About To Change, Get Ready!

I speak blessing to all of you. Get ready to overcome your challenges! Get ready for the financial breakthrough! Get ready for the job you are believing God for! Get ready for the job promotion! Get ready for your healing! Get ready for that mate you are believing God for! Get ready for peace in your marriage! Get ready!!!

Hallelujah, God has already done some marvelous things. Claim it, believe it, and Receive it!!! In Jesus name, Amen!! Amen!!

Scriptures says:

But blessed are those who trust in the Lord and have made the Lord their hope and confidence.

Jeremiah 17:7 NLT

Day 27: Doubt No More

Throughout our lives we have all experienced the feeling of doubt. Truth of the matter is that we must act on faith, not doubt. Doubt is unbelief and it hinders what God wants to do in our lives. "We are people of Faith and we Doubt no more. Let us begin to see and experience all what God has for each and every one of us regardless of what we may be experiencing." Amen!! Amen!!

Heavenly Father, thank you for being patient in our times of doubt! Grant that our doubt be replaced by faith as we continue to wait for your plan to manifest on your schedule, not ours Lord. We pray this in Jesus name. Amen!!!!

Day 28: Who Are We, Really?

You see… the biologist tells us that we are DNA; the evolutionist tells us that we're an ascending animal; the boss tells us we are replaceable; the government tells us that we are a taxpayer and medical liability; your dad calls you daughter/son; your spouse calls you sweetheart, and your kids call you Mommy/Daddy… but every day we need to turn our heart toward heaven and be reminded of who we really are.

We are a child of the One and Only, Almighty God – creator of the universe. We are here for God's good pleasure. We are owned by God; loved by God; filled with His Spirit; guided by His hand; used for His purpose and crowned with His glory! Amen!! Amen!! Amen!!

Day 29: When There Seems To Be No Way

Have you ever faced a situation and said, "It just don't look good. I do not know what to do. There seems to be no way?"

"There is no way I can continue to deal with the pressure at work!"

"There is no way I will be able to handle these bills!"

"There is no way to save my marriage!"

"There seems to be no way the doctor will be able to handle my sickness!"

YOU ARE WRONG!

See, with God's help, there is ALWAYS a way. It may not be easy; it may not be convenient; it may not come quickly. You may have to go over, under, around, or through difficulty—but if you will simply TRUST JESUS and keep on keeping on, you will find a way. Jesus said in John 14:6, "I am the Way and the Truth and the Life." If you Believe the Word of God, then He is the Way, and He will help you find a way even where there doesn't seem to be one.

Father, I thank You that You have "made a way." Help me to focus on You and not on my circumstances. Thank You that You are making a way for me today. In Jesus name, Amen!! Amen!!

Day 30: When It Doesn't Make Sense

It is easy to give your cares to the Lord and trust Him when everything is going like you want it to go.

What happens when there are difficulties in your life, pain in your life, relationship that is nonexistent, something wrong with your body, you need a job, you need some money, or you got a child who need guidance, and you ask, "God, where are you?" Will you Trust Him???

Remember this:

1. God is our source, and He knows everything.
2. He's an on-time God.
3. Just Trust Him.
4. Be Obedient.
5. He will lead you through.

Let us Pray:

Heavenly Father, I ask that you place within me your obedient spirit, and help me to walk by faith and not by sight. I may not understand what you are doing in my life, but I Trust you Lord. In this season, I ask that you place within me your spirit of joy, peace and rest to endure all that comes my way. I decide right now to Trust you. I thank you for clarity, guidance, provision, and strength. In Jesus name, Amen and Amen!!!!

Day 31: God Is...

A Way Maker, Miracle Worker, Promise Keeper, Lifer After Darkness. Our God: that is who He is.

Let us pray:

Thank you, Lord, for making a way when we could not see a way out. If we continue to trust and believe your Word, we will experience all that you so desire for us. We thank you; we glorify you; we magnify you. In Jesus name we pray, Amen!!! Amen!!

Scriptures says:

Grace, Mercy, and peace, which come from God the Father and from Jesus Christ the Son of the Father-will continue to be with us who live in truth and love.

2 John 3 NLT

Day 32: Right Thinking

As believers, *right thinking* is something that is so important we simply cannot live without it. Why? Because many of the problems we deal with in our lives are rooted in *wrong thinking* patterns, which are not based on the truth.

Right thinking is a result of regular, personal fellowship with God through prayer and the Word. It is important for us to come to grips with the fact that our lives will not get straightened out until our thinking gets straightened out. In Jesus name, Amen!

Thoughts bear fruit. When you and I think good thoughts, our lives produce good fruit. When we think bad thoughts, our lives produce bad fruits.

The longer I serve God and study His Word, the more I realize how important it is for me to be aware of what is going on in my mind. Where the mind goes, the man follows. Continually watching over our thoughts is the only way we will ever be able to keep them in line with God's Word and receive our manifestation and breakthrough. Amen!! Amen!!

Day 33: We Must Stop Worrying And We Must Trust God

Scriptures says:

That is why I tell you not to worry about everyday life–whether you have enough food and drink, or enough clothes to wear. Isn't life more than food, and your body more than clothing?

Matthew 6:25

Can all your worries add a single moment to your life?

Matthew 6:27

So, don't worry about these things, saying, 'What will we eat? What will we drink? What will we wear?' These things dominate the thoughts of unbelievers, but your heavenly Father already knows all your needs.

Matthew 6:31-32

26

My brothers and sisters, breaking down these Scriptures simply tells us to stop worrying, stop putting our situations and circumstances over what God's Word says, and start believing and trusting God's Word. In Jesus name, Amen!!!

Finally, the Bible tells us in Matthew 6:33:

> Seek the Kingdom of God above all else, and live righteously, and He will give you everything you need.

If we continue to agree with what God's Word says, then I'm telling you we experience everything that God desires for us. In Jesus name, Amen, Amen and Amen!!!!!

Day 34: Focus On God

If you are Worrying or Fretting about something—your problems, situations, or circumstances—then you are not Trusting GOD. See, what you are doing is putting your situations before God. The longer you Focus on the problem, the larger it becomes. You must put God over the situation. Focus On GOD!!!!!! In Jesus name, Amen!! Amen!!

Scriptures says:

> Give your burdens to the LORD, and He will take care of you. He will not permit the godly to slip and fall.
>
> *Psalms 55:22 NLT*

Day 35: Am I REALLY Trusting God?

The ONLY way to see manifestation in your life is to BELIEVE and TRUST GOD. However, it is difficult—and especially difficult if you are not meditating on God's Word day and night.

Let's say you're looking for a job, and every time you turn around you're getting rejected. Do you feel defeated? Are you really trusting God? Let's say things aren't going well in your marriage or you can't seem to find a mate. Do you feel defeated? Are you really trusting God? Let's say you're experiencing health issues that just have not gotten any better or healed. Do you feel defeated? Are you really trusting God? Let's say you're experiencing financial difficulties or waiting for a business to prosper. Do you feel defeated? Are you really trusting God?

If you feel defeated, worried, and stressed, I can tell you right now you are not Trusting God. Trust Him!!!! In Jesus name, Amen!!!

Day 36: Peace Of Life

Peace is one of the most important elements to enjoying your life. Jesus came so we could have joy, righteousness, and peace.

A life of frustration and struggle, a life without peace, is the result of focusing on things you can't do anything about.

When you worry about things beyond your control, stress and anxiety begin to creep into your life.

Be anxious for nothing, but in everything by prayer and supplication, with thanksgiving, let your requests be made known to God; and the peace of God, which surpasses all understanding, will guard your hearts and minds through Christ Jesus.

Philippians 4:6-7 NKJV

Once we realize we are struggling with something and feel upset, we need to start praying and immediately turn the situation over to God to experience peace. Amen!!! Amen!!!

Day 37: Cast Your Cares, Speak Positive Things

Is there something in your life that you are worried and anxious about???

I encourage you to expect something good to happen in your life, and to expect it on purpose. In Jesus name!

You can choose your own thoughts. You don't have to just think whatever falls in your head. You can cast out wrong thoughts and choose right thoughts. Faith starts in our hearts, as a gift from God, but it is released when we think and speak right things that line up with God's Word.

When we have a problem, we can either do what the devil wants us to do and worry about it, get anxious, and try to figure things out on our own, or we can do what God wants us to do and think about the promises in His Word. In Jesus name, Amen, Amen and Amen!!!!!

Day 38: God Is Bigger

Is God bigger than any health challenges? Yes. Is God bigger than divorce? Yes. Can God handle that problem at work? Yes. Is God bigger than any financial challenge? Yes. Is God bigger than anything you might face in life? Yes. And He longs to be the One you trust, the One to deliver you, the One to strengthen you, and hold you through the storm. Amen!!

See, we need to stand up and lift our hands and declare with our mouths that God is working on our behalf. Just declare that GOD IS BIGGER!!!

Scriptures says:

But Jesus looked at them and said, "With man this is impossible, but with God all things are possible."

Matthew 19:26

Day 39: Experience Hope

Are you in a season right now where you feel like nothing exciting is happening for you? Are you feeling alone, hopeless, or discouraged?

Scriptures says:

I know the plans that I have for you... plans to prosper you... to give you a future and a hope.

Jeremiah 29:11

If you are feeling discouraged today and are having a hard time believing, just know that God is closer to you than you know.

More than likely He is using this season right now to stretch, bend, purify, and refine you into a warrior for the Kingdom.

However, this process may require some crushing, pressing, filtering out the junk, and even sitting for a while to mature, but in due season, it's our time to be released! God has a plan for you and me, and it's probably just around the corner! BELIEVE IT! Amen!!

Day 40: Be Blessed

Scriptures says:

May the Lord bless you and protect you. May the Lord smile on you and be gracious to you. May the Lord show you His favor and give you His peace.

Numbers 6:24-26 NLT

Amen!! Amen!!!!!!!

Day 41: Nothing Is Impossible With God

God designed, created, and sustains all things. He is the one who determined in the first place what is possible and impossible.

We all too easily forget Jesus' words:

> The things which are impossible with men are possible with God.

Luke 18:27

Believe His Word! Today, you may find yourself in a calling from God that seems impossible to fulfill, or you may find yourself in a bad situation that seems impossible to resolve. Despite the difficulties, the barriers, and the impossibilities, do not forget whom you serve.

Do not forget that with the God you serve nothing will be impossible. Amen!! Amen!!

Day 42: You're Not Stuck—You're Going To Make It Through!

We will all go through situations in life—some bad, some good. We may be facing difficulties, but at least we are moving forward.

Scriptures says:

> When you pass through the waters, I will be with you, and through the rivers, they will not overwhelm you. When you walk through the fire, you will not be burned.

Isaiah 43:2

God's Word here is clear: we will go through things, but if we trust Him, He will be right by our side.

We must choose the right attitude toward our challenges and refuse to quit or give up. We may have to do what is right for a long time before we feel it is "paying off," but if

32

we stay faithful and refuse to give up, good results will come.

Decide now to keep going forward, trusting God no matter how difficult it is because you know He will be with you and you will grow in faith as a result. Amen!! Amen!!! Amen!!!!

Day 43: The Lord Will Make A Way

Have you been wondering, "when is God going to make a way for my situation? I have been going through this situation way too long. I just cannot figure it out. I do not know what else to do. Lord where you at?"

Stop stressing, do not worry, stop trying to figure it out, and rest in Jesus. He will make a way.

Do not worry about when it is going to happen or how it is going to happen. Just know that God will make a way.

Didn't God deliver the Israelites out of Egypt? He made a way! Didn't God favor David over Goliath? He made a way! Hasn't God brought you this far? He made a way! So, this is what you need to do:

Trust in the Lord with all your heart and lean not on YOUR own understanding. Seek His will in all you do, and He will make your path straight. In Jesus name, Amen!! Amen!!!

Day 44: The Bible

See, the Bible is The Word of God which does the body, soul, and mind good. There's deliverance in the Word! There's healing in the Word! There's power in the Word! There's knowledge in the Word! There's prosperity in the Word! All in the Bible...

The Bible will remind you that our God is able to take every situation in our lives and use it for our highest good and for His greatest glory.

The Bible also will help you develop a strength that will enable you to overcome sin and temptation.

The Bible can help you love the difficult people in your life.

The Bible can help you find your purpose in life.

For these reasons and for thousands of others... develop an addiction to the Word of God. You will become the person you were made to be when you delight in His Word! THE BIBLE!! Amen!! Amen!!

Day 45: God Is On The Scene

God's promises are pure and true if we Believe it. He never deceives or fails to keep His promises. Never! I know there are times in our spiritual journey that seem dry. We may be convinced that God has forgotten us. We may feel completely overwhelmed by our problems and situation and baffled that God has done nothing to help. Not true! GOD Is on the scene!!

Even though we may grow weary and discouraged and disappointed, we can always depend on God. All we must do is trust and believe that God is truly on the scene. Amen!! Amen!!

Day 46: Doing It God's Way

It is impossible to be neutral when dealing with the spiritual realm. Either we will do things the sinful way (Our Way) or God's way.

The sinful path will be fun for a while but then things are not fun anymore. A lot of pain, heartache, confusion and then no control over our lives which leaves us spiritually dead and could potentially lead us to physical death.

However, God's way is the only way. At first, doing it God's way may look harder than the way of sin, but in due time you will discover that God's way lead to Everlasting Joy, Peace, Manifestation, Breakthrough, Miracles, Healings, Deliverance and Prosperity etc. Amen and Amen!!!!

Scriptures says:

Thus, says the LORD, your Redeemer, the Holy One of Israel, "I am the LORD your God, who teaches you to profit, who leads you in the way you should go."
Isaiah 48:17 NIV

Day 47: God's Power Of Hope

Being disappointed is that gut feeling of just being sick over what might have been... what could have been... what should have been.

"Hope does not disappoint."

When you feel that your life has fallen apart... He meets you there. When you mistakenly believe that you have been defeated one too many times... He is there. HOPE!!!!

We serve an awesome and amazing God who is so powerful that He is working behind the scenes of our lives to take every disappointment we encounter and work it to our advantage.

Although your heart may be heavy with heartache, pain and one downfall after another, hold on to HOPE my brothers and sisters.

You can HOPE in trials, setbacks and disappointment, because God is still on the throne of your life. He is still in control. You have not escaped His love. And... you are not "dis"-appointed. He has got this. He's got you. HOPE!!!!! Amen!! Amen!!

Day 48: It's Time To Change

Are you enjoying the life and blessings of God in your everyday life? Or have you made a series of choices resulting in stress, disappointment, and pain? Do not spend your time and energy mourning all the bad decisions you have made; just start making good ones. There is hope for you!

The only way to experience true change is to do the opposite of whatever you used to do—one choice at a time. You may be in debt because you have made a lot of bad choices with money! You may be lonely because of a series of bad choices in relationships! You may be sick because of a series of unhealthy choices: eating junk food, lack of rest etc.... It is time to change!!

No matter what kind of situations or difficulty you find yourself in, you can still have a blessed life. You cannot do anything about what is behind you, but you can do a great deal about what lies ahead of you. It is time to change!! Amen!! Amen!!

Day 49: Let Go, And Let God!

Let go and let God be your way maker, miracle worker and promise keeper! Let go and let God supply all your needs according to His riches and Glory! Let go and let God give you peace, joy, happiness and comfort!

Truth of the matter is: Things are not going to always work out the way we want them to. We can complain, fuss, stress about it or even do all we feel like we know how, and it is still not enough. We might as well let go of our situations and circumstances and let God be God and it will all work out. Amen!! Amen!!

Commit to the Lord whatever you do, and He will establish your plans.

Proverbs 16:3 NLT

Day 50: God Will Always Be With You

When you go through deep waters, I will be with you. When you go through rivers of difficulty, you will not drown. When you walk through the fire of oppression, you will not be burned up; the flames will not consume you.

Isaiah 43:2 NLT

Day 51: Receive It All

God created and implemented a salvation plan exclusively for you before the foundations of the earth were established. Receive it!!

If you did not know already, you are a part of God's will and family, set apart, chosen, and claimed by God as His very own. By accepting Jesus Christ as your LORD and Savior, receiving His loving gift of salvation, following Him, and AIMING to continuously align yourself with His Word; you are faithfully and actively walking in God's salvation plan for your life as a believer.

Receive all of God's promises for your life today because God's timely salvation is available for you for every area and aspect of your life. It is time to believe, receive, and possess the promises and inheritance our heavenly Father has bestowed on us.

Faithfully obey His instructions, develop in His training, and receive His loving gift of salvation as you triumph in victory, wisdom, and encouragement. In Jesus name, Amen!! Amen!!!!!!

Day 52: We Must Believe!

Why is it that we do not experience our manifestation of whatever we are believing God for? It's simple. We just do not Believe God's Word!!!!

Someone who steals, does not Believe that God will supply all their needs!!

Someone who is always stressed, depressed and angry, does not Believe that God will provide peace and comfort!!

Someone who commits adultery does not Believe the promises of two joining together to become one!!

Someone who does not tithe, does not Believe they can trust God where their finances are concern, and there will be enough!!

Ladies and Gents, we must Believe in order to see manifestation of God show up in our lives. Amen!! Amen!!

Scriptures says:

But those who trust in the Lord will find new strength. They will soar high on wings like eagles.

They will run and not grow weary. They will walk and not faint.

Isaiah 40:31 NLT

Day 53: What Really Matters?

Scriptures says:

Every way of a man is right in his own eyes, but the Lord weighs the hearts.

Proverbs 21:2 NKJV

The world sees you as you appear to be, but God sees you as you really are... He sees your heart, and He understands your intentions. The opinions of others should be relatively unimportant to you; however, God's view of you, His understanding of your actions, your thoughts, and your motivations, should be vitally important.

See, few things in life are more futile than "keeping up appearances" for the sake of others. What is important, of course, is pleasing your Father in heaven. You please Him when your intentions are pure, and your actions are just.

If the narrative of the Scriptures teaches us anything, from the serpent in the garden to the carpenter in Nazareth, it teaches us that things are rarely what they seem... basically, we should not be fooled by appearances. In Jesus name, Amen!!

Day 54: Pressure

Our world is filled with pressures, some good, some bad. The pressures that we feel to follow God's will and obey His commandments are positive pressures. God places them on our hearts, and He intends that we act in accordance with His leadings. But we also face different pressures, ones that are not from God. When we feel pressured to do things or even to think thoughts that lead us away from God, we must beware!

Society seeks to mold us into more worldly beings; God seeks to mold us into new beings that are most certainly not conformed to this world. If we are to please God, we must resist the pressures that society seeks to impose upon us and we must conform ourselves, instead to God's will, to His path, and to His son.

Scriptures says:

For am I now trying to win the favor of people, or God? Or am I striving to please people? If I were still trying to please people, I would not be a slave of Christ.

Galatians 1:10 Holman CSB

Day 55: While Waiting... Who Likes To Wait?

Does it seem like you have been waiting forever for God to come through or move on your behalf? The truth of the matter is this… we all must wait for something! And it is our personal choice whether we will wait well or wait poorly!!!

See, worrying is a waste of time, energy, and emotions.

Do not be negative while you wait. Keep a positive spirit. Do not become bitter while you wait. Do not mistakenly suppose that nothing will ever change for you. Bitterness always turns into selfish anger. Do not whine and complain while you wait. Speak God's Word on your situation.

Here is some ideas; be productive and get involve in healthy activities while you wait! Volunteer somewhere, be an ear to someone who might be experiencing other issues, take someone to lunch, pray for others, worship, get involved in the community/church, or invite people over for dinner and a game night.

While you wait…. Talk the language of hope! Hope should be the native tongue of someone who is waiting. Learn to speak it and receive it while enjoying life at the same time. This demonstrates belief in God. He will see you through. Amen Amen!!!!

Day 56: God Is Always On Time

No matter what you are going through, remember God comes through on time in your victories! Despite the setbacks, holdups, waiting periods, or seasons of perceived stagnations, trust that God is working everything out for your good and has positioned you for greatness for His divine purpose and plan.

As you pursue God, you will experience naysaying ridiculers who doubt God's promises for you and will even laugh at you because you elect to actively trust God in the challenging times and refuse to operate apart from His glorious plan for your life. Do not worry, GOD IS ON TIME!!

Your timely victory is sure to be accompanied with a table prepared for you in the presence of your enemies lacking no good thing! Be encouraged today that although things are not going the way that you desire, Your Divine designer has stitched a custom, exclusive, one-of-a-kind masterpiece and master plan for your life. In Jesus name, Amen!!! Amen!!

Just trust God's Word and believe that God is coming through for you in a timely victory!!!! Amen!!!

Day 57: We Can't Serve Two Masters

Let me explain:

Jesus made it clear that living for personal gain will only lead to great anxiety. Materialism and anxiety are two enemies of spiritual growth. They often work together to lead us away from a balanced life.

We must understand that the essence of life is not found in the possession of things and worrying about the future is never helpful. By ourselves we have little power to change the future, so we must trust God to help us. And God promise to provide for our needs, therefore we have no need to worry. Amen and Amen!!

Scriptures says:

Seek the Kingdom of God above all else, live righteously, and He will give you everything you need.

Matthew 6:33 NLT

Day 58: God's Timely Training

God has a plan, purpose, and will for your life. Despite what people, circumstances, or your thoughts attempt to tell you, remember God knew what He was doing when He divinely ordered your steps as you endured those challenges, sad times, disappointments, setbacks, promotions, expansions, blessings, and positive accelerations.

Your collective life experiences are working together for your good, and training you for the plans, purposes, and will of God. As we journey through life, trusting God is paramount in our lives, although we might not understand all the puzzle pieces.

But when we trust God, knowing that He loves us and will never leave nor forsake us, we are empowered to faithfully believe that God's training is for where He is taking us. The training God has you going through is timed and on purpose! Your training is strengthening you for where God has ordained you to go. No matter what, remember obedience and faith is God's way to the TOP! In Jesus name, Amen and Amen!!

Day 59: The Joy Of God's Word

Are you a depressed Christian? Have you lost your faith? Are you wondering when will I see my breakthrough? You do not have to feel this way. Get in God's Word and experience the joy waiting for you…

During the days of blackness, allow the Bible to become your source of joy and light. During long nights of hopelessness, let the Word of God speak promises and purpose. During months of discouragement, allow the Bible to be a voice of encouragement and blessing.

Something to Ponder: If joy is, indeed, found in His presence, then why do so many of us struggle with staying in a place of joy??????? Answer: NOT BELIEVING GOD.

EXPERIENCE THE JOY OF GOD'S WORD! Amen!! Amen!!

Day 60: Experience The Change

See, most of us want to experience change in our lives, but we are not willing to sacrifice and make the necessary changes. Doing it God way will see us through whatever we may be experiencing.

When we choose to surrender our lives to God and commit ourselves to doing His will, we will experience change and joy. When times get tough God will reveal His path to us and gives us reasons to rejoice.

Making good changes in our lives will not make everyone happy. Some will wonder why we longer relate to them as we did in the past. Some may even criticize us or think we are acting funny. But God is always with us and with His help we will find strength, joy, peace and true happiness in our new life. Amen!! Amen!!

Day 61: Nothing Is Too Hard For The Lord

Are you afraid to ask God to do big things in your life? Is your faith barely there and possibly worn? If so, it's time to abandon your doubts and reclaim your faith in God's promise. Remember, we serve a God of infinite possibilities! But sometimes, because of limited faith and limited understanding, we are led to assume that God cannot or will not intervene in the affairs of the common man. Such assumptions are simply wrong. Always remember that God wants to give us His best! It's up to us to have enough faith in Him to expect it, to feel worthy of it and to accept it! IN JESUS NAME, AMEN!! AMEN!!

Scriptures says:

Is anything too hard for the Lord?

Genesis 18:14 KJV

Day 62: What Must We Do?

Let me explain:

Our investments for Christ in people are critical. Therefore, we must increase our spiritual deposits. Our prayers will live forever before God's throne. Therefore, we must continue to pray, and pray for the generations that may follow. Our testimony may, somehow, live on to inspire another. Therefore, we must live out God's script in faithfulness, excellence, and godliness. Our giving may enable a mission school to thrive, a ministry to grow, a lost one to be found.

Therefore, we must give of what we earn, and give even to sacrifice when we see a need that we can meet. Our children carry our physical and spiritual DNA. We must know that they love and know Him. THIS IS WHAT WE MUST DO!!!!

Consider what lives on when you are gone. Live beyond your life span. Amen!! Amen!!!

Day 63: Start Believing Again

Maybe you are getting tired of being in the situation you are in, only to wonder, "when I will see my breakthrough?" Your Faith is starting to weary, and doubt has set into your mind. I encourage you today my sisters and brothers to Believe Again!!!

Start confessing… I Believe!!

I Believe that God's best is yet to come. I Believe that I am victorious. I Believe that I will overcome. I Believe that God is for me. I Believe that my worst days are behind me. I Believe that something Good is headed my way. I Believe I will reach my destiny. In Jesus name, Amen!!!! I Believe AGAIN!!

Day 64: Slow Down And Enjoy Life

We are some tired folks these days, and proud of it. We work hard, and pay for it with chronic fatigue. We are living in the fast lane, but are we living well?

Majority of the times, we feel like we must grind, bustle, and hustle to obtain all the material things of the world. One may ask: are we victims of the grind, or of poor priorities? Truth be told, those who are weary, stressed, overworked, and overtired hurry along a road of diminishing returns.

We must ask ourselves: how do we obtain true joy, peace and happiness? We display selfish desires to grind and overwork ourselves only to put on the back burner what really matters the most.

The Lord invites those who are weary to rest because we need it! Everything BREAKS DOWN unless you take care of daily maintenance. Back off, and reassess your priorities and ask yourself, "what really makes me happy?"

Abundant living requires more than eight hours sleep – it requires a quieted heart. In Jesus name, Amen!! Amen!!

Day 65: Rejoice In Hope And Experience God's Favor

The Bible is full of hope-filled promises for you and me. We have access to God's presence. He wants to heal us of our diseases. He will supply all our needs. There are so many more. That is why it is so sad when Christians miss out on God's promise due to lack of faith. FAITH IS EVERYTHING!!!

I got a question for you: Don't you want to experience all God's promises? Faith is the key for you to rejoice in the hope of experiencing God's favor on a regular basis.

We can increase in that favor and experience His promises just like Jesus. Even if you do not see those things in your life now, you can rejoice and put your hope in God, knowing that they will come to pass because everything is that is promised in the Bible is for us. In Jesus name. Amen and Amen!!!

Jesus grew in wisdom and stature and in favor with God and all the people.

Luke 2:52 NLT

Day 66: Faith And Victory

Whenever you find yourself faced with a challenge, whether it is physical, financial or relational, apply God's Word and stand on God's Word. If you do this, Victory will manifest and you will experience a satisfaction like no other.

It is so satisfying because when you lay hold of victory by faith in God's Word, you are truly being like Jesus. You are not just getting His blessing; you are living the lifestyle He lived. You are living by faith, just like He did. You are being His disciple! Amen! and Amen!

Scriptures says:

The righteousness of God is revealed from faith to faith. I live by faith.

Romans 1:17

Day 67: Hanging Tough

We are pressed on every side by troubles, but we are not crushed. We are perplexed, but not driven to despair. We are hunted down, but never abandoned by GOD. We get knocked down, but we are not destroyed...

For our present troubles are small and won't last exceptionally long. Yet they produce for us a glory that vastly outweighs them and will last forever! So, we do not look at the troubles we can see now; rather, we fix our gaze on things that cannot be seen. For the things we see now will soon be gone, but the things we cannot see will last forever.

2 Corinthians 4:17-18 NLT

Day 68: Relevance Of God's Grace

To be relevant means to be connected. Better yet, how significant is God in your life? What significance does God play in your life when you get a bad doctor report, you on the verge of divorce, you have debt, you cannot pay your bills, you lost your job, or you are emotionally distressed. Ask yourself, "how significant is God in my life?"

See, most of us feel like we do not need God unless we are close to death or when we need help with a particular situation or circumstances.

Truth of the matter; God should be relevant in our everyday lives whether we are doing good or bad. If God is at the center of it all, your marriage, your career, your health, your emotions, and your finances then "He will fix it." Amen!! Amen!!

Day 69: The Armor Of God

My brothers and sisters, we need to make sure that each piece of God is operating in our lives. Truth, righteousness, faith and prayer will protect us against all strategies of the devil. If we do this, we will sure be able to endure our trials, situations, and storms of life. Amen!!! Amen!!!

Scriptures says:

Be strong in the Lord and in His mighty power. Put on all God's armor so that you will be able to stand firm against all strategies of the devil.

Ephesians 6:10 NLT

Day 70: How Are You Responding?

See, Faith is a positive response of what Grace (Jesus) has made available. This is how you receive victory and manifestation. In other words, when you Believe whatever it is you may be experiencing will come to pass, you will respond in line with your beliefs that it is done.

Now, Faith is not you trying to get God to give you a positive response. Faith is your positive response to what He has made available (deliverance, healing, and prosperity) Faith does not move God. Faith moves you into position to receive what God has already made available.

For example, let us say you go to the doctor and was diagnosed with a sickness. How do you respond? The first thing you say is: "Thank you Lord for my healing and give me wisdom to know what to do." That is how a person respond who genuinely Believe God's Word. But if you say, "Oh Lord Jesus, I do not know what I am going to do, why me Lord?" See, now you ARE RESPONDING WRONG and operating in unbelief and this does not work. Amen!! Amen!!!

Scriptures says:

And Jesus said unto him, "Go thy way; thy faith hath made thee whole."

Mark 10:52 NLT

Day 71: God's Wisdom

There is nothing—absolutely nothing! —on this earth that is as valuable to you as the wisdom of God. It is the key that opens every good door. Prosperity and success. Health and long life. Peace and security. All of these are available to those who learn from and live by the wisdom of God.

But, oddly enough, many believers do not seek God's wisdom until their backs are against the wall.

Learn to seek His wisdom, to listen for His instructions on the little, everyday matters of life. That way, when the big problems come, you will be ready. You will be in the habit of hearing from heaven.

Scriptures says:

I hearken to wisdom, and I dwell securely and in confident trust. I am quiet without fear or dread of evil.

Proverbs 1:33, AMP

Day 72: Stop Complaining, Be Thankful

Complaining is a corrupt form of conversation that causes many people a great deal of problems in their lives. It also opens many doors for the enemy. Words are containers of power. Complaining, grumbling words carry destructive power that will steal your peace and joy.

When we complain about our current situation, we remain in it; when we praise God in the midst of difficulty, He raises us out of it. In Jesus name, Amen!

The best way to start every day is with gratitude and thanksgiving. Get a jump on the devil. If you don't fill your thoughts and conversation with good things, he will definitely fill them with evil things. Truly thankful people do not complain. Amen!! Amen!!

Scriptures says:

But Jesus replied, "stop complaining about what I said."

John 6:43

Day 73: God Did Not Say It Would Be Easy, But He Did Say He Would Be With Us

- I told you that no man will be able to withstand you
- I told you where your feet trod, I give you the land
- I told you if you weather the storm you make it out
- I told you I will bless you going out and coming in
- I told you if I would be with Moses, I would be with you
- I told you that I shall not lie

But I did not tell you that it would be easy.

My dear brothers and sisters, no matter what the situation may look like, no matter what obstacles we must overcome, just know that if we continue to believe the Word and trust God, then victory is ours even if it's not how we imagined!!!!!!!

Scriptures says:

This is my command- be strong and courageous! Do not be afraid or discouraged. For the Lord your God is with you wherever you go.

Joshua 1:9 NLT

Day 74: Thanks For Your Help, Lord!

God's help is always available, but it is only given to those who seek it.

No matter what you may be facing today; Death in the family, Financial troubles, Job security, Marital issues, Depression etc.... Cast all your cares to the Lord, Trust and Believe that He will see you through... Then you will experience PEACE, JOY, and COMFORT. God's help is always available. Amen!!

Scriptures says:

Ask, and it will be given to you; seek, and you will find; knock, and it will be opened to you. For everyone who asks receives, and he who seeks finds, and to him who knocks it will be opened.

Matthew 7:7-8 NKJV

Day 75: A Relationship With God

When you mention God, most people automatically think "religion," which is often defined by traditions, rules, and expectations. The truth is, God has not called us into religion. He has called us into a RELATIONSHIP.

As with any relationship, the more time you spend together, the deeper and more fulfilling the relationship becomes.

For example when you're dating or trying to get to know a person, you spend countless number of times with that individual to really get to know them personally. Same principles apply with God.

Having a real, intimate relationship with God means spending time with Him. God longs to spend time with us. He desires us to journey with Him. Commit to spending some time each day to read the Bible (God talking to you) and pray (you talking to God). You will be blessed as your relationship with God deepens and grows. Amen!! Amen!!

Scriptures says:

Seek the Kingdom of God above all else and live righteously and He will give you everything you need.

Matthew 6:33 NLT

Day 76: We Must Exercise Our Faith For Manifestation

Scriptures says:

For indeed we have had the good news [of salvation] preached to us, just as the Israelites also [when the good news of the promised land came to them]; but the message they heard did not benefit them, because it was not united with faith [in God] by those who heard.

Hebrews 4:2 AMP

This Scripture simply says that when you hear the Word of God and you do not believe what it says it will not work. Bible says faith without work is dead. Now this does not mean you are trying to do something to get God to do something.

Ok. You go to church to hear the Word, but you are only in spirit and faith when you are at church. But you must continue with the Word out of church. For instance, at work, at home, at a party etc.... But to do this you have to pray, praise Him, study God's Word, and meditate daily.

If you want God's promises to manifest in your life you must implement Faith when applying the Word of God. You must become a doer of the Word and not just a hearer of the Word. Amen!!! Amen!!!

Day 77: God Wants You To Know Today: Don't Give Up!

If you are battling with an illness in your body... Don't Give Up!! If you are battling with your finances... Don't Give Up!! If you are battling with a relationship or your marriage... Don't Give Up!!! If you're battling with your employment or schooling... Don't Give Up!!!! If you are battling with your children... Don't Give Up!!!! If you are battling with an addiction... Don't Give Up!!!!! No Matter What Your Battle Is, Don't Give Up!!!!!!

Scriptures says:

Therefore, my dear brothers, stand firm. Let nothing move you. Always give yourself fully to the work of the Lord, because you know that your labor in the Lord is not in vain.

1 Corinthians 15:58

Day 78: Faith In the Midst Of A Storm

Scriptures says:

But soon a fierce storm came up. High waves were breaking into the boat, and it began to fill with water. Jesus was sleeping at the back of the boat with His head on a cushion. The disciples woke Him up, shouting, "Teacher, don't you care that we're going to drown?" When Jesus woke up, He rebuked the wind and said to the waves, "Silence! Be still!" Suddenly the wind stopped, and there was a great calm. Then He asked them, "Why are you afraid? Do you still have no faith?"

Mark 4:37-40 NLT

See, majority of the times we say we have Faith and we Believe the Word of God. "But Do We?" No matter what storms we face in life, if we genuinely believe the Word and Trust God, then Victory is Ours!!!!!!!! In Jesus Name, Amen!!! Amen!!!

Day 79 God's Got You Covered

When you do not get what you expect... God got you covered!!! When you go through disappointments... God got you covered!!! When it seems like things are not getting better... God got you covered!!! When you run into trials and tribulations... God got you covered!!! When you are battling health challenges... God got you covered!!! When

it seems like you're alone… God got you covered!!!
Whatever you may be experiencing, God got you covered!!!

Trust Him. Believe Him. Stay with Him. Enjoy Him. Love
Him. Praise Him. God got you covered!!! In Jesus name,
Amen!! Amen!!

So be strong and courageous! Do not be afraid and
do not panic before them. For the Lord, your God
will personally go ahead of you. He will neither fail
you nor abandon you.

Deuteronomy 31:6 NLT

Day 80: Stay Rooted And Grounded

Stability is an important issue for all of us. Jeremiah 17:8
and Psalm 1:3 both instruct us to be like trees firmly
planted. We are to be well-balanced and temperate (self-
controlled) to keep Satan from devouring us. To withstand
him, we must be rooted, established, strong, immovable
and determined in Christ.

Jesus is the best soil to be rooted in. You can depend on
Him to be stable, the same Jesus all the time, always
faithful, loyal, true to His Word and nature. He does not
change with circumstances, so if you are rooted in Him,
you will not either.

Will you be rooted in the world? Your emotions? Your
circumstances? Your past? Or will you choose today to
plant yourself in Christ? I encourage you to depend on Him
and this way you will experience all that He has for your
life. In Jesus name, Amen!!

60

Day 81: Stay In Peace

Let us talk: See, the storms of life come to us all, but God promise us we can have peace in the storm. Just because we are in a stressful situation does not mean we have to be stressed out, worried, and angered. You may be in the storm, but the key is do not let the storm get in you.

If we allow our situations and circumstances to control us, then we will become a roller coaster. Up one minute and down the next. God wants us to be stable, not moved by the circumstances.

When we are faced with adversity, the best thing for us is to have peace, which mean we are truly trusting that God will work it out no matter how it's look. When we believe, then there is peace and rest that comes upon us.

Scriptures says:

And the peace of God, which transcends all understanding, will guard your hearts and minds in Christ Jesus.

Philippians 4:7 NKJV

Day 82: Faith Brings Victory

No matter what difficult situation you may be facing today, God can turn it around! The doctors may have told you there is no hope. Your bank account may be empty and the creditors knocking on the door. There may be trouble in your family or at your job. You may have a loved one headed for prison. Your problems may be stacked so high, you feel like you can never overcome them. But do not let the devil fool you. Faith Brings Victory!!!

Think about that! If you will dare to believe God's Word, you can have light during a dark world. Faith Brings Victory!!!

"But you can't do it by dragging around in an attitude of defeat."

If you want to walk in constant victory, you must develop a spirit of faith and persevere when the devil is putting pressure on you. Faith Brings Victory!!!!

Faith believes God's Word just because God said it—whether natural circumstances seem to agree or not. People with the spirit of faith always receive the blessings of God. They may go through tests and trials, but they come out victorious every time. Faith Brings Victory!! In Jesus name, Amen!!!!!

Scriptures says:

I have the spirit of faith!

2 Corinthians 4:13

Day 83: You've Been So Good, Lord!

Let us pray:

Father, thank you for the source of hope, which fill me completely with joy and peace because I trust you. Lord I realize I can do nothing apart from you. Lord if you are for me, then who can ever be against me. Thank you, Jesus, Lord I will always be joyful and never stop praying and be thankful in all circumstances. Lord I put my confidence and trust in you because of my faith, without faith I cannot please you. But I can do all things through Christ which strengthens me. In Jesus name, Amen!!!

Day 84: It's Done!

Let us Pray:

Lord Jesus, You're the High Priest of my confession. You are the administrator over the words I have spoken to this situation (whatever the situation is). I want You to know I appreciate it. I thank You for being my Lord. I am standing on the living Word of God and I refuse to change my stand. I know the Word of God will never change. God will never change. The blood of Jesus will never change. The Name of Jesus will never change. So that means the devil and this situation will have to change. Lord God, I thank You for it. From here on, I CONSIDER THIS PROBLEM SOLVED!!! Amen.

In Jesus name, Amen!!!!

Day 85: Prayer Of Peace

Let us pray:

Father, today I want to just thank you. Father forgive me for running after the temporary peace the world offers. I stand before you today knowing the inheritance Jesus left me is priceless and beyond comparison to any material possessions. Holy Spirit, teach me how to activate and use my inheritance of peace, show me what I need to root out of my heart so that I can create space to cultivate a peaceful heart. Open my eyes to see Jesus in the Scriptures I read every day so that I can grow in my knowledge of His greatness, faithfulness, and His character.

Holy Spirit, help me to operate in the measure of peace that Jesus operated in so that I may see countless miracles in my life and those around me, let fear, anxiety, and worry have no room in my life as the peace of God expands in and around me. In Jesus name, Amen and Amen!!!!

Day 86: I Will Praise The Lord

Ladies and Gentlemen, Thanksgiving and praise are integral parts of prayer. When you BELIEVE you RECEIVE, then you begin to praise God for the answer. You thank God that it is done for you.

Thanksgiving and praise involve more than just speaking lovely words to God. There is power in the praise of God. Praise was ordained by God for a definite reason. It serves a purpose.

Whatever adversity is challenging you today, begin to praise God and the peace and victory that Jesus bought for you will be yours. Amen!!

Scriptures says:

I praise the Lord with my whole heart. I show forth all His marvelous works.

Psalm 9:1

Day 87: Keep Your Eyes On Jesus

See, you must believe that God will make a way out, even when you do not see a way out. Just because you cannot see a way out, does not mean God can't make a way out. So, if you believe this, you will continue to Study God's Word and Praise Him!!

When the enemy tries to get you to quit: Keep your eyes on Jesus! When it seems like the bottom has fell out: Keep your eyes on Jesus! When it seems like you do not know up from down: Keep your eyes on Jesus! When it seems like God is taking forever to come through: Keep your eyes on Jesus!! Amen!!

Scriptures says:

Keep your eyes on Jesus, who both began and finished this race we are in. Study how He did it. Because He never lost sight of where He was headed–that exhilarating finish in and with God–He could put up with anything along the way: Cross, shame, whatever.

Hebrews 12:2

Day 88: God Is Faithful

As men and women of God we will have to endure many trials as well as tribulations. It is literally one test after another with each one preparing you for the next. But nevertheless, He has promised that He will remain faithful

65

to us, yes FAITHFUL TO US, as His Word says that He will never leave us nor forsake us. Because regardless of the situation, you can stand on the fact that it is for your good and for His glory!

Scriptures says:

Yet if any man suffers as a Christian, let him not be ashamed; but let him glorify God on this behalf.

1 Peter 4:16 KJV

You will come out better than you were before...

Day 89: Destined To Win

My brothers and sisters, you are made to win. You are destined to win. God has given you everything you need in Christ in order to excel and succeed at life. Believe it and Receive it! Why? Because you are destined to WIN!!!

See, you might be feeling weak now. The enemy is on your trail bringing all kinds of distraction and disease. The enemy wants you to give in, but I am here to let you know that you have the victory in Jesus name. You cannot give up now. What you have been praying and believing God for is getting ready to manifest. Amen!! Amen!!

Scriptures says:

But thanks be to God! He gives us victory through our Lord Jesus Christ.

1 Corinthians 15:57

Day 90: Wait On The Lord

Scriptures says:

But blessed are those who trust in the Lord and have made the Lord their hope and confidence. They are like trees planted along a riverbank, with roots that reach deep into the water. Such trees are not bothered by the heat or worried by long months of drought. Their leaves stay green, and they never stop producing fruit.

Jeremiah 17:7-8 NLT

Now, if you really stop and think about what this Scripture says you will understand; even if you must endure some trials or tribulations in your life, you still will be blessed in the process and that is amazing. Because no matter what you may be going through God is still God and He will still provide. In Jesus name, Amen!!

All you must do is Believe and apply what this Scripture is saying. If you trust God, you will endure to the end. Meaning you will be blessed and while you are going through the storm or storms, He's right by side keeping you until Victory is yours. Amen!! Amen!!!

Day 91: God Has Already Answered Your Prayers

Scriptures says:

I tell you, you can pray for anything, and if you believe that you've received it, it will be yours.

Mark 11:24 NLT

This is a powerful Scripture. Most of us pray asking God to move on our behalf and when we do not see instant results we feel as if our prayers are not being answered.

See, when we go to God in prayer; God hears us the first time. In order to agree with what the Scriptures says we must genuinely believe what we are praying for will come to pass no matter what our current situation is looking like.

Whatever it is that you are praying about, I encourage you today to start focusing on the ANSWER to your prayer not the problem. UNBELIEF is what stop MANIFESTATION to your prayers!!!!! Amen! Amen!

Day 92: Trust The Word

Since God has never commanded us to do anything without providing us with the ability to do it, we can be sure He has given every believer the power to accomplish and overcome in any and every situation.

Nothing you do by the power of God is hard. You can make it hard by trying to do it in your own strength. But if you will learn to rest in God through faith in His Word, the struggle will disappear.

You see, if you will trust God's Word, that Word will fight for you in any area of life. You will not have to wrestle your problems to the ground and solve them with your own great willpower. All you will have to do is OPEN your BIBLE and start speaking out God's Word about the situation. Release your faith in that Word and it will conquer any problems. That's right! God's Word will work miracles in your life... Amen!! Amen!!!

Now the God of hope fill you with all joy and peace in believing, that ye may abound in hope, through the power of the Holy Ghost.

Romans 15:13 KJV

Day 93: God's Got Your Back

When you go through deep waters, I will be with you. When you go through rivers of difficulty, you will not drown. When you walk through the fire of oppression, you will not be burned up; the flames will not consume you.

Isaiah 43:2 NLT

In Jesus name, Amen!!! Thank You Lord!!!!!

Day 94: Rest In Jesus

Having an attitude of peace and calm is priceless. It is an attitude that says, "I'm resting and trusting God," and it speaks powerfully to people. But it takes time, focus, and the grace of God to be consistently resting in the finish work of Jesus.

Too often our stress level is tied up in our circumstances. You could be stressed because you are always busy, or you are struggling financially or because you are not getting along with someone you love.

To conquer the stress in our lives, we need to learn to REST IN JESUS.

God, I know that You have overcome any and every obstacle, so I ask You to help me live in the peace that You've provided for me. Show me how to trust and rest in You as I live "in the now." Amen!! Amen!!! Thank you, Jesus!

Day 95: Extremely Close!

Have you been experiencing Trials, Troubles, Jealously and Envy? I am here to let you know that you are close to what God has in store for you! You're close to your Overflow! You are close to your Miracle!!

Have you been experiencing Confusion, Problems and Enemies? Just believe that you are Extremely Close to your Victory!! Amen!! Amen!!

Scriptures says:

For the Lord, your God is He who goes with you to fight for you against your enemies, to give you the victory.

Deuteronomy 20:4 NIV

Day 96: Meditate On It

Scriptures says:

But they delight in the law of the Lord, meditating on it day and night. They are like trees planted along the riverbank, bearing fruit each season. Their leaves never wither, and they prosper in all they do.

Psalms 1:2-3 NLT

Think about this Scripture for a second; Mediating on God's Word day and night will allow you to become grounded in His Word which will allow you to Prosper in all you do. This is radical information, Ladies and Gentlemen.

Now, I must say; there is a difference between meditating on the Bible and reading the Bible.

The Psalmist made it quite clear that meditating on God's Word brings results. As you ponder who God is and what He's saying to you, you will grow. Believe in God's Word and begin to Prosper in everything. It is really that simple. In Jesus name, Amen!!

Day 97: God Will Protect

Even when I walk through the darkest valley, I will not be afraid, for you are close beside me. Your rod and your staff protect and comfort me.

Psalms 23:4 NLT

No matter what we may be experiencing right now in our lives God will protect and bring us through. All He is asking us to do is Believe that He will do what His Word says no matter how challenging our situations may be... Amen!!! Amen!!!

Day 98: We Can Do It!

Scriptures says:

For I can do everything through Christ, who gives me strength.

Philippians 4:13 NLT

Just ponder on this Scripture for a second; No matter how hard things may get. No matter if you lost a loved one. No matter if you are dealing with a health challenge. No matter if you face financial challenges. No matter what the challenges may be. You have the strength to make it through by Jesus Christ.

We must understand that the Scripture did not say we can do anything we want because of our experience, college

72

degrees, smarts, mental toughness, or hard work. No, we can only do it when the power of Christ works through us. Nothing is too difficult if God is leading the way. "Let God lead, and WE CAN DO IT." In Jesus name, Amen!!!! Amen!!!

Day 99: Be Strong

Life can come at us from all different directions in many ways that causes confusion, stress, discomfort, and anxiety. But if we keep our eyes on Jesus, then we will prevail. Amen!!

I encourage you today my sisters and brothers to Stay Strong, Stay in God's Word, Believe His Word, and Act on His Word.

Scriptures says:

This is my command-be strong and courageous! Do not be afraid or discouraged. For the Lord God is with you wherever you go.

Joshua 1:9 NLT

Day 100: Is Your Faith Weak?

Ask yourself, "is my Faith weak, or am I not using it?" See, a lot of us really do not have a Faith issue. What we have is a "Use Issue." We start out good but when troubles come, we begin to waiver. The reason why manifestation has not showed up is because we are not continuing to utilize our Faith on a consistent basis.

The Bible tells us that Peter was doing simply fine walking on water while keeping his eyes on Jesus as he walked. As soon as the winds started blowing, Peter took his eyes off Jesus and begin to sink. Peter started out with awesome Faith, but he did not stick with it. As a result, he started sinking and Jesus reached down to take him in the boat.

Ladies and gentlemen, no matter how hard your circumstances may be, I encourage you to continue to exercise your Faith until you see your Breakthrough and Manifestation. Keep that Faith Working!!! In Jesus name, Amen!!

Day 101: God's Way

Have you ever thought that you may be having trouble experiencing your breakthrough because you are still trying to do things your way instead of God's way??

Just like in mathematics in school, if you have the wrong equation, you will always get the wrong answer.

This is because God works in ways that we cannot even understand; the Bible says that His ways are higher than our ways. So instead of looking at our circumstances with "common sense" or trying to get the approval of others' opinions, we should have faith in God and God only to lead and direct us. Then He will guide us to who, when, and where. In Jesus name, Amen!! Amen!!!

Day 102: Where Is Your Confidence?

Insecurity is the opposite of confidence. Insecurity is a profound sense of self-doubt; a deep feeling of uncertainty about our basic worth and our place in the world. Often, we assume that the solution is to get better at self-belief and convince ourselves that we are not as bad as we feel.

The truth is the only solution to our insecurity is to get a deeper understanding of the God who created you because your worth is found in Him. "Get That Confidence."

Scriptures says:

My heart is confident in you, O God; my heart is confident. No wonder I can sing your praises!

Psalms 57:7 NLT

Eventually we need to find greater weight in God's Word for us, and believe that He's chosen us and chosen to love us, despite what others SEE, HAVE SAID, or DONE. In Jesus name, Amen!! Amen!!

Day 103: Don't Give Up Hope

When you have hope, you have a supernatural expectancy that what God has promised will come to pass in your life. But you got to believe it!!!

When you are so locked in on the Word of God, you cannot be distracted from it, Divine hope will come alive in you.

When your hope gets that strong, it does not matter what kind of unbelief, opposition, or situation contrary to the Word the devil tries to throw your way. It just bounces off you. Because you genuinely believe whatever it is your hoping and believing God for.

So, whatever you are believing God for, get your supernatural expectancy up for it. Eagerly long for it. Stretch your neck out and refuse to be distracted by all the worldly things that would get you off course. Keep the promise of God's Word before your eyes and that will keep your hope up, and you will see your desire come to pass! Amen!!!

Scriptures says:

According to my earnest expectation and my hope, that in nothing I shall be ashamed, but that with all boldness, as always, so now Christ shall be magnified in my body, whether it be by life, or by death.

Philippians 1:20 KJV

Day 104: Help Is Here!

Many people have received Jesus as Savior and Lord. They will go to heaven, but never draw on the full capacity of the Holy Spirit that is available to them or experience the true success God wants them to enjoy on Earth. They might be on their way to heaven but will not enjoy the trip.

Too often we look at those who have wealth, position, power and we consider them "successful." But many people who are considered successful still lack peace, joy, contentment, and other true blessings. Such people have never learned to depend completely on the power of the Holy Spirit.

We know God wants to help us because He sent a Divine Helper, the Holy Spirit, to live inside us.

We often struggle needlessly because we do not receive the help available to us. I encourage you to depend on Him, not on your own strength. Whatever you are facing, you do not have to go through it alone. HELP IS HERE!!!! In Jesus name, Amen!!!!

Day 105: Display God's Type Of Love

God does not just love the lovely. He loves the unlovely too. No matter how bad or mean someone might be, if they will turn to Him, He will cleanse them and forgive them.

That is the way God loves us, and that is the way He expects us to love each other.

It is God's love that sets you apart. We will have to stop centering our lives on what we want and what we feel. We will have to stop looking out for ourselves all the time. Walking in love means we lay down our own rights and look out for the other person's rights instead. Amen!! God will surely Bless!!

Not only that, when you stop being selfish, you will be a happier person. We are not made to live that way. We are not big enough or powerful enough for everything to center around us. The more we keep our minds on ourselves, the easier it is for the devil to upset us. Guess what? You can keep your mind on obeying His Word and living a life of love! He will take care of everything else. Amen!!! Amen!!

Scriptures says:

Love is patient and kind. Love is not jealous or boastful or proud or rude. It does not demand its own way. It is not irritable, and it keeps no record of being wronged.

1 Corinthians 13:4-5

Day 106: Pray And Give Thanks

Giving thanks is so important to being able to hear God's voice because, like praise and worship, it is something God responds to. It is something God loves, something that warms His heart. Anytime we give God pleasure like that, our intimacy with Him increases, and that makes for a better relationship with Him.

No matter what we pray for, thanksgiving should always go with it. Amen!!!

I encourage you to examine your life, to pay attention to your thoughts and your words, and see how much thanksgiving you express. If you want a challenge, just try to get through an entire day without uttering one word of complaint. Develop an attitude of thanksgiving in every situation.

Speak words of thanksgiving, not words of complaint. Amen!! Amen!!

Day 107: God's Word Is For Real

The Word of God is true even when everything else around you are telling you otherwise. You will never get in a situation where you exercise faith in God's Word, and God fails to keep that Word. Never!

Understand, however, that it is not enough just to know what the Word says. It must be reality to you—more real than the problems, challenges and circumstances you face.

That is why we must constantly center ourselves on God's Word, because it is that Word that produces faith in our hearts. In fact, you cannot deepen your faith in God without deepening your trust in His Word. Let God be found true... if you believe in His Word, it will come to pass. Amen! Amen!

Scriptures says:

Of course not! Even if everyone else is a liar, God is true. As the Scriptures say about Him, "You will be proved right in what you say, and you will win your case in court."

Romans 3:4 NLT

Day 108: The World Vs. God

The world will often lead you astray, but God will not. His counsel leads you to Himself, which of course is the path He has always intended for you to take. Are you facing a difficult decision, a troubling circumstance, or a powerful temptation? If so, it is time to step back, stop focusing on the world, and to focus instead on the will of your Father in heaven.

A man's heart plans his way, but the Lord directs his steps.

Proverbs 16:9 NKJV

Lord, help us to make decisions that are pleasing to you. Help us to be honest, patient, thoughtful, and obedient. Above all, help us to follow the teachings of Jesus, not just today, but every day. Amen!

Day 109: God's Gift

People often wonder, what am I supposed to do with my life? What is my purpose for being alive? Does God have a plan for me? One way God answers these questions is through our natural gifts and abilities. He leads us to understand our purpose through the skills and talents He gives us.

A God-given talent, or what we often call "a gift," is something we can do easily, something that comes naturally.

If you are not sure of your purpose in life, just do what you are good at and then watch God confirm your choices by blessing your endeavors. Do not spend your life trying to do what you are not gifted to do.

When people work in jobs where they are not gifted, they are miserable, and so is everyone around them.

If we do what we are good at doing, we will sense God's anointing (presence and power) on our efforts. We will know we are operating in our gifts and that doing so honors God and ministers life to others. God speaks to us through this anointing, giving us peace and joy to know we are fulfilling His plan for our lives. Amen!!! Amen!!!

Day 110: Let The Past Stay In The Past

We have all had those times in our lives when we were expecting something to happen or work out the way we wanted it to, and it did not, only to leave us disappointed and even hopeless at times. Let it go!!!!

You thought the relationship would work out, or you were in line for a promotion, or an opportunity seem to be available, and these things did not go as planned. Let it go!!

When things do not go as you planned them, quit standing there and rehearsing and nursing the problems. This is not the end of the world, no matter how you feel about it. How you respond is the key to overcoming this moment. WOW!!!!! That is Powerful.

Today, decide to let go of the past so that you can begin to embrace the new thing that God has in store for you. Do not spend any more time re-living or rehearsing the thing that happened in your past. You cannot fix it or change it. The best thing to do is let it go. In Jesus name, Amen and Amen!!!

Day 111: Let's Continue To Change

Scriptures says:

Beloved, now are we the sons of God, and it doth not yet appear what we shall be: but we know that, when He shall appear, we shall be like Him; for we shall see Him as He is.

1 John 3:2 KJV

Just ponder on this Scripture for a minute.

Sometimes you do not think like a child of God. Sometimes you do not act like a child of God. Sometimes you do not love like a child of God. But you are still being changed. Let us continue to Change.

Sometimes it takes pain and heartache to get God to take you where He wants you. But all in all, we are still being changed. Let us continue to seek God and watch the change occur in our lives. Amen!!

Day 112: God Is With Us

Scriptures says:

When you go through deep waters, I will be with you. When you go through rivers of difficulty, you will not drown. When you walk through the fire of oppression, you will not be burned up; the flames will not consume you.

Isaiah 43:2 NLT

Ponder on this Scripture for a second. If we genuinely Believe the Word of God, then what is with all the stressing, worrying and frustration? In this passage God simply explain to us that He got us no matter what we have been through or going through.

Ok. Here is the problem. We are putting our problems and situations over the Word of God. Just cannot do it!! We are leaning on our understanding instead of God's understanding. Just cannot do it!! We are not studying and meditating on God's Word ENOUGH to Believe His Word. Just cannot do it!!

Let us continue to pray, study and meditate on God's Word. This way we will have a better understanding of what the Word of God says. God is with us. He has gone ahead of our situations and problems and worked them out. But we got to Believe it. Amen!!! Amen!! GOD IS SURELY WITH US!!!!!!!

Day 113: Godly Relationship

See, God is calling us for a relationship with Him. Only then will we experience the goodness of the Lord.

See, a wedding is an experience, but a marriage is a relationship!! Having a baby is an experience, but raising a child is a relationship!! People look for experience, but God is calling us for a relationship.

When we open our heart to a real relationship with God through Christ, we learn to trust, believe, and act on God's Word to encounter God best for our lives. Amen!!! Amen!!!

Trust in the Lord with all your heart, do not depend on your own understanding. Seek His will in all you do, and He will show you which path to take.

Proverbs 3:5-6 NLT

Day 114: Seasons

We all must endure a season in our lives, but the good news is that seasons do pass by.

I know we understand: without God, there is no hope during life's battles. If He is not fighting our battles with us, we will be overwhelmed by the spiritual forces arrayed against us and it will seem like the season will never pass by.

Here are five critical words to remember when enduring a season: AND IT CAME TO PASS. See, whatever your IT is, in due time it will pass by. Just continue to praise God, be patient, and watch Him work. Amen!! Amen!!

Scriptures says:

"For I know the plans I have for you," says the Lord. "They are plans for good and not for disaster, to give you a future and a hope."

Jeremiah 29:11 NLT

Day 115: It's Your Decision, It's Your Answer, What Will You Choose?

Let me explain:

84

Did you know that your decision to seek a deeper relationship with God will not remove all the problems from your life? In fact, it will bring about a series of personal crisis as you constantly seek to say "yes" to God although the world encourages you to do otherwise.

Now, each time you are tempted to distance yourself from the Creator, you will face a spiritual crisis. Life here on earth can now be one test after another, and with each crisis comes yet another opportunity to grow closer to God... Or to distance yourself from His plan for your life.

Today, you will face many opportunities to say "yes" to Him, and you will also encounter many opportunities to say "no." Your answers will determine the quality of your day and the direction of your life, so answer carefully, very carefully.

The Christian life is not simply following principles, but being empowered to fulfill our purpose... knowing and exalting Christ. In Jesus name, Amen!!!!

Day 116: Bitterness Hinders Hearing

Bitterness toward God is a sure hindrance to hearing His voice. Anytime bitterness tries to take hold of you, refuse it.

When we get hurt, we must realize that every person has a free will, and we cannot control that free will, even through prayer. We can pray that God will speak to people who may hurt us or cause some sort of strife in our lives; we can ask Him to lead them to do right instead of wrong, but the bottom line is that He must leave them to make their own choices. If someone makes a choice that hurts us, we should not blame it on God and become bitter toward

Him. We trust God's Word that it will work out for our good.

God's Word for you today:

If you get hurt, do not ever blame God. He is the best friend you have. Amen!! Amen!!!

Scriptures says:

Do not fear, for I am with you; do not be afraid, for I am your God. I will strengthen you; I will help you; I will hold on to you with my righteous right hand.

Isaiah 41:10

Day 117: Just Give It To God

Even though we may be suffering greatly, we can have confidence that God answers our prayers. God always hears our petitions. We should all be as bold as David, who claimed victory immediately after finishing his prayer. When we seek God and surrender our lives to Him, we can pray with assurance and declare victory because God himself will overcome our enemies.

God will protect us if we are willing to admit our weaknesses and wholeheartedly depend on Him. He will give us the power to do what is right in difficult situations and give us the ability to walk without stumbling.

Scriptures says:

Yet I am confident I will see the Lord's goodness while I am here in the land of the living. Wait patiently for the Lord. Be brave and courageous. Yes, wait patiently for the Lord.

Psalm 27:13-14 NLT

Day 118: Trials and Tribulations

The purpose of trials is so you can tell others:

- I have seen Him.
- I know Him.
- He is good.
- He is real.
- He saves.
- He heals.
- He delivers.
- He changes.
- He transforms lives.

Scriptures says:

Dear brothers and sisters, when troubles of any kind come your way, consider it an opportunity for great joy. For you know that when your faith is tested, your endurance has a chance to grow. So, let it grow, for when your endurance is fully developed, you will be perfect and complete, needing nothing.

James 1:2-4 NLT

Day 119: Praise God In Your Prison

Hold on! Let me explain.

Sometimes we find ourselves in such horrible messes that it is hard to imagine waiting one more second. "Where is God? When is He coming through to help me in this mess I am in?" Truth of the matter is, God has already fixed it if we believe it is fixed. But we need to Trust Him with a sweet and simple faith. Then, in a way we never could have figured out, God moves suddenly!

See, Paul and Silas knew about waiting, and they waited well. Acts 16 tells the story of how they were attacked by a crowd, beaten and thrown in jail. Verse 24 says the jailer put them into the inner prison (the dungeon) and fastened their feet in the stocks.

Paul and Silas decided to start singing, and began to worship the Lord as they waited on God. Suddenly, God sent an earthquake that opened the prison doors and loosed their chains. Paul and Silas believed and trusted God. He set them free!

When we patiently and expectantly wait on God during our trials, situations, and circumstances, suddenly God breaks through. So, do not give up! Do not stop believing! Stay full of hope and expectation. God's power is limitless, and He'll breakthrough for you. Amen!!! Amen!!!

Day 120: Do You Want To Be Happy?

The truth can hurt you or the truth can change you. It depends how you respond. Putting God at the center of it all is key to joy. Do you want to be happy???

See, you can cry yourself to sleep, put stress and pressure on yourself, punch a hole in the wall, cuss and fuss, yell as loud as you can, or even drink to ease the pain. This will not change a thing until you understand. Do you want to be happy?????

Are you tired of asking God when and why? Are tired of going in circles? Does it appear nothing is changing? Does it seem like it is getting worse? It is time for you to get out the way, Believe the Word, and let GOD take the wheel, SO YOU CAN BE HAPPY!!!!!!

Scriptures says:

The gatekeeper opens the gate for him, and the sheep recognize his voice and come to him. He calls his own sheep by name and leads them out. After he has gathered his own flock, he walks ahead of them, and they follow him because they know his voice.

John 10:3-4 NLT

Day 121: Let Not Your Heart Be Troubled

People everywhere—many believers included—are running around wringing their hands, worrying about what to do. But there is really no need for it. After all, Jesus has already told us what to do when we are having an untroubled heart even in the most troubling times:

"ABIDE IN ME."

When you abide in Jesus, He is not just your Sunday God. He is not just the One you think about when you get in trouble. No, when you abide in Him, He is your Monday Lord. He is your Tuesday Lord. He is your Wednesday, Thursday, Friday, and Saturday Lord. He is your daytime Lord and nighttime Lord.

When you rest in the Word all day long like that, then the Word begins to abide in you, and it will constantly teach you the ways and wisdom of God. It will keep your heart from being troubled.

Scriptures says:

I do not let my heart be troubled because I trust and abide in Jesus.

John 14:1

Day 122: Just Trust!

Scriptures says:

Trust in the Lord with all your heart; do not depend on your own understanding. Seek His will in all you do, and He will show you which path to take.

Proverbs 3:5-6 NLT

What a promise!!! God will direct us and crown our efforts with success if we put our Trust in Him rather than try to do it on our own. Putting God first means turning our lives and wills over to Him. Surrendering to His lordship is humbling, but He will surely bless us as a result... In Jesus name, Amen!!

Day 123: Don't Worry, God Will Bring You Through!

Whatever you may be going through, remember Jesus is Lord.

When you say Jesus is Lord, that means He is OVER everything. He is OVER your Storm, He's OVER your Troubles, He's OVER your Rough Season. Do not you know that God is not going to let you fall or faint in whatever you may be going through? GOD is going to bring you out!! Amen!!

Scriptures says:

I'm singing joyful praise to GOD. I'm turning Cartwheels of Joy to my savior God. Counting on GOD'S Rule to prevail, I take heart and gain strength. I run like a deer. I feel like I'm king of the mountain!

Habakkuk 3:17-19 MSG

Day 124: The Lord Is With You

Understand this my dear brothers and sisters: no matter what you may be experiencing or what your current situation looks like, just know that God is with you!!

You may be wondering how your circumstances is going to work out for you, or wondering when God is going to come through. He has already gone ahead of you. He is working it out. You got to trust Him. When you trust Him, then you will understand He is with you and He has been with you all the while. You were just trying to do things your way, and you could not see God's way. Amen!! Amen!!

This is my command–be strong and courageous! Do not be afraid or discouraged. For the Lord, your God is with you wherever you go.

Joshua 1:9 NLT

Day 125: Put Your Faith In God

Ask yourself today, "What am I doing with my faith?" Are you putting your faith in yourself, or in others, or in your circumstances? That is not living in grace, that is just living by your own strength and works. And it will not get the job done!

But when you release your faith and trust God to do what you cannot do; you are putting your faith in Him.

Put your faith in God. He wants to give you His grace today.

Let us Pray:

God, I know that life will not always go the way I want it to, but I trust in You. By faith, I receive Your grace, the power You have freely given to help me walk through any situation I face today. Amen Amen!!!!!!!!!

Day 126: Wait With Patience

Many people want change, but they do not want to go through the waiting process. But the truth is, waiting is a given, we are going to wait. The question is, are we going to wait the wrong or right way? If we wait the wrong way, we will be miserable; but if we decide to wait God's way, we can become patient and enjoy the wait.

One thing I will say: it takes practice, but as we let God help us in each situation, we develop patience, which is one of the most important Christian virtues. Patience is a fruit of the Spirit. It is developed only under trial, so we must not run from difficult situations.

As we develop patience, the Bible says we finally feel completely satisfied, lacking nothing. Even our relationship with God involves progressive changes. We learn to trust Him in a deeper way by going through many experiences that require us to wait longer than we would like.

Trust me, the waiting may be hard, but it will make you stronger. The benefits that patience brings are certainly worth any uncomfortable wait!

Scriptures says:

Wait patiently for the Lord. Be brave and courageous. Yes, wait patiently for the Lord.
Psalm 27:13-14 NLT

Day 127: Practice God's Word Instead Of Being Religious

Let me explain:

Developing a relationship is a process with God. You might know someone who just cannot seem to get right. But the correct way is to love them, pray for them, and do not condemn them. We all have sinned!!!!

We must understand that God's Grace is available to everybody that Believes. However, it is a choice to Believe, which we understand. But see, if we going to act like Jesus... Jesus loved a woman who was caught in an adulterous act, as well as been with several men. Jesus was a friend to sinners.

See, the key is learning how to love ANYBODY, so that the goodness you show will help cause them to change. Tell them your testimony. Tell them how God delivered you, healed you and changed your life. Tell them!!!

See, you cannot help changing nobody's life by always bringing up the past, pointing out flaws, or condemning them. Just love them, pray for them, and watch God work and the changes that makes because they see a mirror image of God. Amen!!! Amen!!!

Day 128: Watch Him Move

Your confession is what you say—not just with your lips, but with your actions. Jesus is the High Priest of your confession. That means He has the authority to bring to pass anything you confess by faith that is in line with His Word. That is what He was sent by God to do.

That means when you are broke, and you confess by faith, "My God supplies all my needs according to His riches in glory by Christ Jesus," (Philippians 4:19), Jesus has the authority to deliver to you the necessary finances. Or, when you are sick and you confess by faith, "I'm healed by the stripes of Jesus," you put yourself in a position to receive that healing from Him.

We as God's people should say what God says about us, instead of what our circumstances says.

The reason that seems strange to most of us is because we are so selfish. We want to see everything from our own viewpoint. But when you confess the Word instead of your circumstances, you are laying down your own viewpoint and speaking from God's viewpoint instead.

So, speak God's words over your circumstances today. Speak His words in faith... and watch Him move!

Scriptures says:

I am strong in the Lord and in the power of His might.

Ephesians 6:10

Day 129: The Battle Has Been Won

Remember that old song: *Victory is mine; Victory is mine; Victory today is mine. I told Satan, get thee behind, Victory today is mine.*

However, for this to manifest in your life, you must believe it, regardless of what your situation and circumstances say. Claim the victory over your situation, and watch how things begin to change. Amen!! Amen!!

Scriptures says:

But thanks be to God! He gives us the victory through our Lord Jesus Christ.

1 Corinthians 15:57

Day 130: Don't Quit

"We are Christian, We go to Church, We Pray, We stay in the Word of God. We feel like we're just not getting anywhere. We are as weak as when we first accepted Christ as our Savior. We still fail. We just don't know if it's worth it. By now we should know all the right things to do, but we don't do them. What kind of Christian are we?"

"Probably a growing Christian."

But if we were not growing, we would not lament our failures; we would be satisfied about our spiritual level, or tell ourselves how good we are.

If we are not careful, we allow the devil to point to what we have not accomplished and where we have been weak. When that happens, it is easy to feel bad or want to give up. That is not the way of the Spirit. No matter how much we mess up or go through various storms in our lives, God does not give up on us.

"Don't quit. Don't give up."

Scriptures says:

Fear not, for I have redeemed you; I have called you by your name; you are Mine. When you pass through the waters, I will be with you, and through the rivers, they will not overwhelm you. When you walk through the fire, you will not be burned or scorched, nor will the flame kindle upon you.

Isaiah 43:1b-2

This is God's promise. He does not promise to take us completely out of troubles or hardships, but He does promise to be with us as we go through them. And when God is with us, what is there to worry about? Amen!! Amen!!

Day 131: Open Your Mouth

See, when we pray, and make positive confession and praise God, the devil will flee. It's when we keep our mouth closed with worrying, anxiety, and stressing that the devil has full control.

No matter what you may be facing or going through, open your mouth!! When all hell is breaking loose in your life, open your mouth!! When you are stressed out, open your mouth!! When you cannot see your way out, open your mouth!! When you feel like giving up, and things does not make sense, OPEN YOUR MOUTH!!! Amen!! Amen!!

Day 132: We Shall Overcome!

All of us have either faced difficult times, are facing difficult times, or will face difficult times. Just maybe once or twice you have felt like throwing in the towel and giving up on God and your faith.

Now, if we are truly trusting God, we are not responsible for the ultimate outcome of difficult times. Even when things do not turn out the way we want or expect, God is still God.

All we need to do is believe, trust, and we will have the power to obey God's Word. The great news is that our ability to overcome does not come from our own strength; it comes from the power of Holy Spirit. Which means we shall overcome. Amen!! Amen!!

Day 133: God's Love Is More Powerful Than Abuse

Abuse means: "to misuse, to use improperly, to use up, or to injure by maltreatment." The effects of abuse can be devastating and long-lasting. Many people never recover from it.

There are different kinds of abuse: church abuse, relationships abuse, job abuse, sexual, emotional, verbal,

98

physical. No matter the form, the results are always stressful and terrible. It will keep you from functioning properly and prevent you from seeing, receiving and experiencing the righteousness, peace, and joy of God's kingdom.

If you have been abused in the past, understand today that God loves you. Nothing can separate you from His love. He has made a way for you to be free from your past and to enter true Kingdom living.

Let us pray:

God, I've been abused and misused, but I won't let my past affect my future. Overwhelm me with Your love today so that I can experience Your freedom from abuse. Amen and Amen!!!!

Day 134: Get The Word On It

Let me explain:

Go find the Word (Scriptures) that covers your situation. You may be stressing, struggling with an addiction, financial concerns, relationships etc. Whatever the issues may be, just find God's Word on your situation, and this means you have GOD on your situation, and you are covered if you believe the Word.

For instance, it is just like your insurance policy. When you're covered, you're good; when you are not covered, you have all kinds of issues. However, the key to getting God on your situation is simply believing His Word. Amen!! Amen!!

Your Word is a lamp to guide my feet and a light for my path.

Psalms 119:105 NLT

Day 135: Unbelief

One of the greatest enemies of real faith is what is called "unbelief." People who operate in unbelief read the Word and think they believe it. But when pressure comes, they do not act on it.

Unbelievers say, "I believe the Bible from cover to cover. I believe I'm healed by the stripes of Jesus because the Bible says so." But when sickness comes and attacks their bodies, they stop saying, "By His stripes I'm healed!" and start saying, "I'm sick."

Real faith believes what the Word says even though eyes and feelings say something different. Faith does not care what the symptoms are. It does not care how the circumstances look. It is not moved by what the banker says, or the doctor, or the lawyer, or the bill collector.

Faith in God's Word will change the symptoms. It will change the bank. It will bring the money to get the bills paid. Faith will turn every defeat into victory. It is God's success formula! But you must give that faith an opportunity to work. You must keep God's Word in your mouth and meditate on it in your heart.

Scriptures says:

But do not just listen to God's Word. You must do what it says. Otherwise, you are only fooling yourselves. For if you listen to the Word and do not obey, it is like glancing at your face in a mirror. You see yourself, walk away, and forget what you look like.

James 1:22-24 NLT

Day 136: Want To Experience God's Peace?

Scriptures says:

Do not let your heart be troubled, Trust in God, and trust in me.

In John 14:1

Scripture plainly tells us to trust God and Jesus, and we have the power to do so no matter what we may be going through. It is our choice, though.

Scriptures says:

I have told you these things, so that in me you may have peace. In this world you will have trouble. But take heart! I have overcome the world.

John 16:33

This Scripture tells us that we will have trials and tribulations, but in order to overcome, we must trust God's Word. If you are worried, stressed, angered, and tired, then you do not have peace and you are not trusting God's Word. Trust God and Experience Joy and Peace!!! Amen!! Amen!!

Day 137: Prayer Of Peace And Encouragement

Lord Jesus, give me a revelation in my heart today that knows You are good! Father, I get weary and worried, and I need You to pour out Your peace into my life right now. Please give me the reassurance to keep moving forward even when I am not feeling like it. Please bring people into my life who will speak truth and encouragement when I am feeling discouraged. I give all my life to You, and I ask that You do whatever it takes to build my faith. Use me for Your Kingdom! I love You, Lord! In Jesus Name, Amen!! Amen!!

Day 138: Seeking God

If we have gone through life trusting in our own judgment, we may find it hard to surrender to God and His plan for us. But if we refuse to seek God's help and direction, we may never know just how good He can be to us. He has the power and the wisdom we need to have victory in our struggles with sin and temptation. Amen!! Amen!!

Scriptures says:

Taste and see that the Lord is good. Oh, the joys of those who take refuge in Him!

Psalm 34:8 NLT

102

Day 139: Be Patient, Watch The Goodness Of The Lord

The Lord is good, mighty and everlasting. All we must do is trust in His Word and watch. Amen!!

Scriptures says:

I waited patiently for the Lord to help me, and He turned to me and heard my cry. He lifted me out of the pit of despair, out of the mud and the mire. He set my feet on solid ground and steadied me as I walked along. He has given me a new song to sing, a hymn of praise to our God. Many will see what He has done and be amazed. They will put their trust in the Lord.

Psalm 40:1-3

Day 140: God's Word Makes Sense

As we learn about God through His Word, we learn of His ways, so it seems only logical that we should do all we can to follow it. We got to Believe it to follow it.

This is a significant part of seeking out God's will for us. In the Bible, God has left us guidelines for how He expects us to live. He has also promised that He will help us to carry out His will if only we will ask Him.

Studying, pondering, and applying God's Word should become a joyful experience that will implant God's truth firmly in our heart and mind. Amen!! Amen!!

Day 141: Let Jesus Lead The Way

We need to be receptive and responsive to what Jesus is doing in our lives and WE need to get out the way and let Jesus be Jesus. Instead of us trying to force Jesus to do what we want, when we want it, we need to relax and experience what He is already doing.

See, we need to be patience by waiting and trusting God's timing. Such awareness helps us live responsively, ready to do God's will.

Truth of the matter, we fail to see the many blessings the Lord has provided because of our situation and circumstances, as well as being so busy looking for other things our way.

We must trust the Lord enough to let Him lead instead of us. When two people trying to lead, often there is confusion, conflict, anxiety, resentment, etc. Let God be God as we follow His lead, as He guide us gracefully through our lives. Amen!!! Amen!!

Scriptures says:

Don't act thoughtlessly but understand what the Lord wants you to do.

Ephesians 5:17 NLT

Day 142: Rejoice Always

When your mind is going down an unpleasant, gloomy path, stop it in its tracks and remind yourself to rejoice.

It is important not only to be joyful, but to think about specific reasons for rejoicing. They can be as simple as God's daily provisions for you: food, shelter, clothing. Relationships with loved ones can also be a rich source of Joy.

Choosing to rejoice will bless you and those around you. It will also strengthen your relationship with the Lord.

Scriptures says:

Rejoice in the Lord already. I will say it again: Rejoice!

Philippians 4:4 NIV

Day 143: Don't Worry, Trust God And Believe

True happiness can be found in any situation of life when we recognize that God is at work. Because Christ is within us, we can act calmly in the face of painful and difficult situations. Real peace comes when we focus on God.

The more we commit ourselves to knowing God's will through prayer and the study of His Word, the better prepared we are to help ourselves to Trust His Word and continue to grow spiritually. Amen!!

105

Don't worry about anything; instead, pray about everything. Tell God what you need and thank Him for all He has done. Then you will experience God's peace, which exceeds anything we can understand. His peace will guard your heart and mind as you live in Christ Jesus.

Philippians 4:6 NLT

Day 144: Just Follow Jesus

When you choose to follow Jesus, it is you simply saying yes to His will and to His direction, nothing more or nothing less.

However, if you genuinely want to follow Jesus, then you must let go of everything that is holding you back from fully clinging to God, no matter how good some things seemed. Whether they are habits, people, or opinions, you must let go and fully embrace God's way of living, His opinion of you, and the right people to fit your new lifestyle.

This way you will experience all that God has for you.

Following Jesus is a lifelong adventure that shapes and forms you from the inside out. It will come at a cost; it will take you denying yourself and embracing Gods how. So today and each day you live, choose to follow Jesus. Amen!! Amen!!

Day 145: Sharing The Gospel

There is something powerful about hearing testimony from those who have been through incredible storms and/or are still going through the storms of life. We all like to hear about the happy outcomes, which is always encouraging.

I believe that one of the most powerful ways we can share the Gospel with others is how we connect it with our own stories. A powerful tool of evangelism is not just sharing the good news of Jesus that we see in the Bible, but doing it in a way that connects the good news of Jesus with our own story and journey of faith!

When we share with people what our lives were like before Jesus; and now that Jesus lives among us, it makes the Gospel come alive, and ignites fires of hope and healing!

When we learn to trust, it produces testimony which shows the world the good news of a loving, gracious Father! That is THE GOSPEL! Amen!! Amen!!

Day 146: The Lord Will Provide, The Lord Has Provided

Ladies and Gentlemen, this is something to give God praise for. Not only will the Lord provide, but He has also already provided. No matter what you maybe experience or going through, Lord almighty has already provided for your situation. All you must do is believe it.

In the Bible, God called Abraham to sacrifice his son Isaac. Three things are needed for this sacrifice: fire, wood, and a lamb. As they continued their journey, Isaac looked around to see that they had fire and wood, but no lamb. He asked his father: where is the Lamb? Abraham stated: God will provide. See, Isaac did not realize *he* was the sacrifice, but his father Abraham trusted and believed God would provide regardless of the current situation. True belief was demonstrated.

Understand, my brothers and sisters, that God already has everything worked out even before we can see or understand. It is up to us to believe it. Amen!! Amen!!

Scriptures says:

And this same God who takes care of me will supply all your needs from His glorious riches, which have been given to us in Christ Jesus.

Philippians 4:19 NLT

Day 147: Be Confident In His Medicine

Use God's prescription for health, troubles, situations, and uncomfortable circumstances to work in your life. Do not be discouraged if you do not see immediate results.

Do not let lingering symptoms cause you to doubt. After all, when you go to the doctor, you do not always feel better right away. The medication he/she gives you often takes some time before it begins to work. You do not allow this delay to discourage you, so do not allow God's timing to discourage you either. When you take God's medicine, you are really "treating" your spirit, which is the source of it all.

As soon as you begin to take God's medicine, realize that the moment you begin to take it, (the Word of God) the healing process begins.

Remember: your confidence is in God's Word, His medicine... not in your symptoms (situation, troubles, circumstances, etc.). Amen!!!! Amen!!!!

Day 148: It Will All Work Out

Ladies and Gentlemen, we must believe and come to have great confidence in God's ability to work things out. No matter what is going on or how lowly our situation appears to be. We got to BELIEVE God is always working things according to His great sovereign plan.

It is imperative that we do not put our situations and circumstances above almighty God. This will only cause more Pain, Anger, Stress, and Frustrations.

Whatever you may be dealing with, you can rest assured that God has plans to work things out. God is working all things after the counsel of His own will. So relax! Remember what the Word of God says!!

Scriptures says:

Commit everything you do to the Lord. Trust Him, and He will help you.

Psalm 37:5 NLT

I waited PATIENTLY for the Lord to help me, and He turned to me and heard my cry.

Psalm 40:1 NLT

Day 149: Don't Doubt, God Will Bring You Through

A lot of times when things do not go the way we planned, fear and doubt begins to settle within us. Do not let it, God will bring us through.

See, personal troubles have a way of causing us to doubt our calling, our faith, and our God. Thankfully, we have a Lord who understands our weakness. And He promises us the mercy and grace that we need to fulfill our journey. Amen!! Amen!!

Scriptures says:

Show me the right path, O Lord; point out the road for me to follow. Lead me by your truth and teach me, for you are a God who saves me. All day long I put my hope in you.

Psalm 25:4-5 NLT

Day 150: Trust God Through The Storm

Jesus walked on water, and then empowered Peter, through faith, to do the same. Life is never without its occasional storms. However, when we trust God, we—like Peter—can receive God's power to make it through the storm, In Jesus' name.

Ladies and Gentlemen, if we hold onto our faith and keep our eyes on Jesus, we will not be overcome by the storms of life, no matter the storms we face!!!!!! Just continue to put God above the storms.

It is when we focus on the troubled waters around us, and forget God's assistance, that we begin to sink. If we want to make continued progress, we need to keep our eyes on God.

Scriptures says:

Faith is the confidence that what we hope for will happen; it gives us assurance about things we cannot see.

Hebrews 11:1 NLT

Day 151: The Word Of God Works

The Word Of God works... if you apply the Word of God. The only way to apply the Word is to study, meditate day and night, and Believe the Word.

See, people think the Word Of God doesn't work, but the true issue is: people don't work the Word of God.

If you want to see breakthrough and manifestation come to pass, Ladies and Gentlemen, I encourage you today to get in the Word, study the Word, believe the Word, apply the Word, and WATCH IT WORK!!!! Amen!! Amen!! In Jesus name, Amen!!

Scriptures says:

I pray that God, the source of hope, will fill you completely with joy and peace because you trust in

Him. Then you will overflow with confident hope through the power of the Holy Spirit.

Romans 15:13 NLT

Day 152: Have The Attitude Of Christ In This World

Many people today are living in a perpetual state of overload, stretching themselves to the limit. As a result, they are on the verge of collapse. Even the atmosphere seems to be charged with all kinds of stress, pressure, discouragement, and negativity.

But the good news is that we serve a God who is bigger and tougher than anything we may endure. We do not have to operate by the world's system, reacting like the world. Our attitude and approach should be entirely different. TRUSTING THE WORD OF GOD. Point blank!!!

The world responds to difficulties by being stressed, upset, and discouraged, but if we are trusting God then we do not need to allow ourselves to be agitated, disturbed, stressed, or upset about our situations or circumstances.

I have noticed that the right attitude and approach can completely turn a situation around. The right attitude opens the door for God to work supernaturally and help you to overcome whatever it is you may be experiencing.

Let us pray:

God, I choose to trust you, even during this world, I choose to respond with Your peace and the mind of Christ. Amen and Amen!!

Day 153: Do Not Be Discouraged

Whatever you may be experiencing, I encourage you to continue to keep faith and stay in God's Word.

It is easy to give in and give up, only to realize that you still will encounter trials and tribulations even after you have given up. So do not give up; be encouraged.

Here is the key: Pray, study, and Believe God's Word, and you shall be encouraged.

Scriptures says:

This is my command: be strong and courageous! Do not be afraid or discouraged. For the Lord God is with you wherever you go.

Joshua 1:9 NLT

Day 154: Why Does A Good God Let Bad Things Happen?

When we experience tragedy, being angry with God is quite common. People frequently ask, "If God is good, all-powerful, and full of love for us, why didn't He stop the thing that caused the pain?"

This is where Satan seeks to build a wall between God and the hurting person. He seizes the opportunity to say, "God isn't good, and He can't be trusted." However, we know according to the Word of God, the truth is not in Satan, he is a liar and the father of lies.

Read James 1:17. Everything good comes from God. God is good, and He cannot be anything else. Furthermore, He is not one way one time, and another way another time. He does not change. He is good, and that is the way He is.

It is obvious that God does not always stop tragedy, and we honestly do not always know why bad things happen. First Corinthians 13:12 says, "…Now I know in part (imperfectly)…." We must remember that faith will always require us to accept unanswered questions, and we must come to the place where we are satisfied to know the One who knows, and place our trust in Him.

Let us pray:

God, I may not always understand why bad things happen, but I know that You are good. When I do not understand why, I will find my comfort in You. Amen!! Amen!!

Day 155: Changing And Renewing The Mind

"If you want to see change then you have to make a change."

If you continue to do something the same way, then you will continue to get the same results.

Scriptures says:

Do not copy the behavior and customs of this world, but let GOD transform you into a new person by changing the way you think. Then you will learn to know GOD'S will for you, which is good and pleasing and perfect.

Roman 12:2 NLT

114

Day 156: The Purpose Of Doing It God's Way

Okay, first you must ask yourself: What do I know about this amazing God? Do I believe in God? Do I accept the Bible as it reveals that God exists and Jesus came and rose on the third day?

See, God, He works mightily in and through those who BELIEVE HIS WORD.

When we embrace God with our whole heart and worship Him with our whole life, then what happens is: we begin to experience the inner fruit of the Spirit that transforms our lives from the inside out. When we are growing, experiencing restoration in our relationships and doing the right thing, it is evident that God is in us and with us.

As a result of this, we begin to spread His Word. We demonstrate true love. We recognize the full personhood of others and respect boundaries. We look out for the rights, preferences, and comfort of others. We begin to value and enjoy others.

Then: For any situation, relationship, or decision we face, we can rest assured that over time, it will lead to blessings in the form of fruit such as Joy, Peace, Favor, Victory, Healing, and Prosperity. And most importantly, God gets the Glory!!! Amen!!! DO IT GODS WAY, IT PAYS OFF!! TRUST ME, Amen!!

Day 157: Be Blessed And Stay Blessed

Scriptures says:

But blessed are those who trust in the Lord and have made the Lord their hope and confidence. They are like trees planted along a riverbank, with roots that reach deep into the water. Such trees are not bothered by the heat or worried by long months of drought. Their leaves stay green, and they never stop producing fruit.

Jeremiah 17:7-8 NLT

This Scripture is one of many Scriptures that gives us the blueprint to being blessed and staying blessed as we experience trials and tribulations. We must Trust God's Word and we shall overcome. Amen!!! Amen!

Day 158: Keep Your Faith Working

The Bible tells us in Matthew 14:28 that Peter walked on water for a short stint if he kept his eyes on Jesus. But then the wind and waves hit, and he took his eyes off Jesus and began to sink. Why? Because he did not keep his faith working.

See, a lot of times we think we do not have enough faith, but that is not the issue at times. We need to keep it going and keep believing.

Likewise, no matter how long it takes for whatever we are believing God for; we must keep our faith working. No matter the storms and difficulties of life, we must keep our faith working. As soon as we take our eyes off Jesus we will sink as well.

Let us keep our eyes on Jesus and experience all that God has for us. Amen!! Amen!!

Day 159: Give Your Cares To God And Follow Your Heart

When we veer off the course that our heart is advising us to follow, we can make our lives difficult.

Now, I am not talking about selfish desires; I am talking about pursuing the desires that God puts in your heart. What do you want out of life? What do you believe is God's will for you? Are you pursuing it?

Some people have too many cares and worries that keep them from stepping out and following what is in their heart. They have decided it is out of their reach.

The Bible says we should cast all our cares upon God, for He cares for us. Whatever worry you have that is keeping you from following your heart, you need to give it to God and let Him take care of it.

Let us pray:

God, sometimes I do not pursue what You've placed in my heart because of my worries and cares, so today, I give them to You. I know You can handle them, and You want me to be free to follow my heart. In Jesus name, Amen!!!

Day 160: Learn To Trust God's Plan For You

You can simplify your life by learning to develop trust in God. Far too often, we don't allow ourselves to trust.

It is easy to get stressed out and run-down trying to make your life work on your own, but that never works. And God's plan is always better than your own.

Trust grows as we take steps of faith and experience God's faithfulness.

Trusting God brings a supernatural rest to our souls, allowing us to live simply and freely, the way He wants us to live. So even when it does not make sense, trust Him, and experience His freedom and rest.

Let us pray:

Father God, your ways are better than mine and I know that trusting in my own strength will get me nowhere. I place my trust in You. Even when it does not make sense to me, I choose to trust You, knowing You will make Your plans come to pass. In Jesus name, Amen!! Amen!!!

Day 161: Giving Your All To God

Many people want to receive from God, but they are not willing to give all of themselves to Him.

Give yourself to God. Give Him everything you are, everything you hope to be, all your dreams, visions, hopes and desires. Make everything His, and He will demonstrate His power through your life.

Let us pray:

God, today I give You my all: my hands, my mouth, my mind, my body, my money, and my time. Everything I have is Yours. I want to do Your will today. In Jesus name, Amen!! Amen!!!!

Day 162: How To Make Your Way Prosperous

Scriptures says:

Study this Book of Instruction continually. Meditate on it day and night so you will be sure to obey everything written in it. Only then will you prosper and succeed in all you do.

Joshua 1:8 NLT

This Scripture is just as plain as it wants to be. It says follow God's Word, spend time in God's Word, and Believe God's Word, and you shall make your way Prosperous.

However, it did not say "do what you want to do and how you want to do it, and you will be prosperous." Here is the issue: we want God's blessings without following God's Word. It does not work that way no matter how hard you try.

Do it God's way and watch how joyful your life becomes. In Jesus name, Amen!! Amen!!

119

Day 163: Struggling With Unbelief?

Scriptures says:

Immediately the father of the child cried out and said with tears, Lord I believe, help my unbelief!

Mark 9:24 KJV

Even when you feel distant from your creator, God is never distant from you. When you sincerely seek His presence, He will touch your heart, calm your fears, and restore your faith in the future...and your faith in Him.

Let us pray:

Dear Lord, when I am filled with uncertainty and doubt, give me faith. In the dark moments of life, keep me mindful of your healing power and your infinite love, so that I may live courageously and faithfully today and every day... In Jesus name, Amen!

Day 164: Wait On The Lord

See, you probably saying: Wait? How much longer do I have to wait? I have been waiting. I am getting weary. Where are you Lord? I have been praying, studying and believing. How much longer? My Brothers and Sisters I am here to let you know that the Lord has not forgotten you. Just continue to wait. He will see you through.

Whatever you may be experiencing right now, wait on the Lord! You may be experiencing financial difficulties. Wait on the Lord! You and your spouse may be having marital issues. Wait on the Lord! You need a breakthrough. Wait on the Lord! You need healing. Wait on the Lord. I encourage you today, whatever you have been praying to God for, just continue to Wait!!!

While you wait, continue to Pray, Study God's Word, Be a Blessing to others, Believe God's Word, and remain in Peace. Amen!! Amen!!

Scriptures says:

Wait patiently for the Lord. Be brave and courageous. Yes, wait patiently for the Lord.

Psalms 27:14 NLT

Day 165: Change Is Good

If you continue to do the same things over and over, then you will get the same results. In order to get different results, then you must change. If we want to experience God's best for our lives, then we must CHANGE!!!

Think about this for a second:

What if for one week we exchanged our mobile phone for our Bible? Anywhere we normally take our phone, we take our Bible instead. Anytime we normally look at our phone, we look at God's Word instead. The time we spend calling, texting, and browsing online with our phone is traded for time reading Scripture. Aww man, the difference this exchange would make in our lives in just one week would be radical. Change will begin!!!

We will begin to see things differently. We would start to really apply more of God's way versus the World way. Real happiness, comfort and peace will begin. This way we can change not only our lives but the lives of those around us. This gives God the Glory and that is what He wants. Also, in exchange we can begin to experience all that He has for our lives. In Jesus name, Amen!!!

Day 166: Focus And Trust

If you are Worrying or Fretting about something, then you are not Trusting GOD. The longer you Focus on the problem, the larger it becomes. Focus On GOD!!!!!!

Scriptures says:

Give your burdens to the LORD, and He will take care of you. He will not permit the godly to slip and fall.

Psalms 55:22 NLT

Day 167: No Matter What, Continue To Praise The Lord

No matter what you've been through, no matter what you are going through, give God praise!!!

Scriptures says:

I will praise the LORD at all times. I will constantly speak His praises.

Psalms 34:1 NLT

Day 168: Rise Above!

"Life is like a Ship with water all around it. If the Water gets in the Ship, then the Ship will sink."

There are all kinds of storms, problems, distractions, sins etc. that is happening around us. But if we keep our focus on God, and do not let those things "Get in us," then we shall not Sink, and we will continue to "RISE ABOVE All!" Amen! Amen!

Day 169: Victory Is Mine!

Whatever you're going through, you're going to come out Victorious on the other side!!!!!

Scriptures says:

Now thanks be unto God, which always causeth us to triumph in Christ, and maketh manifest the savour of His knowledge by us in every place.

2 Corinthians 2:14

Day 170: Put It In God

Scriptures says:

Why am I discouraged? Why is my heart so sad? I will put my hope in God! I will praise Him again– my Savior and my God!

Psalms 43:5 NLT

It only makes sense to give all our cares to God, praise Him during our battles and watch what happens. We think we can fix our issues and situation all by ourselves. We cannot unless God is involved.

This Scripture says: Why am I discouraged? Because you trying to do it your way without God FULLY being involved. Why is my heart so sad? Because the way you trying to do it has not turned out the way you wanted it to over a period. I will praise Him again. See, God must be included while you wait for the battle to be won. Keep Pressing On, Praising God and Responding POSITIVE. Amen!! Amen!!

Day 171: God's Best Is Coming

What do you mean "God's best is coming?" Think about this Scripture for a minute:

124

May the Lord lead your hearts into a full understanding and expression of the love of God and the patient endurance that comes from Christ.

2 Thessalonians 3:5 NLT

See, if we allow God to lead us, we can begin to develop an understanding of His love for us, Patience for whatever we may be experiencing, and the promises God has for us.

During our spiritual journey, God will give us more along the way than when we first started. Why? Because He wants us to exercise our faith and start. We might not start out seeing the results we are hoping for in our situation or circumstances, but if we continue to pray, Believe, and respond positive, our blessings begin to show up and show out. Give it all to God, Stay with Him and GOD'S BEST IS COMING!!! In Jesus name, Amen!! Amen!!

Day 172: Keep Your Mind On Jesus

Man, what a powerful true statement... See, in order to endure whatever we may be experiencing, we must keep our mind on Jesus. We must meditate on His Word day and night. I am not talking about just memorizing Scriptures, which is fine. Listen: quoting Scriptures will not feed you. You must do more like studying, meditating; believe and live the Word out to be spiritually fed. This allows us to keep our mind on Jesus.

When everything you have tried fails... Keep your mind on Jesus! You get a negative report from the doctor... Keep your mind on Jesus! Are you experiencing financial challenges? Keep your mind on Jesus! Having marital issues? Keep your mind on Jesus! Trying to break an addiction? Keep your mind on Jesus, and all will work out for your good. In Jesus name, Amen! Amen!!!

Day 173: It All Makes Sense, Even If It Seems Cloudy

God is in control of our World. He created it and the laws that govern it. It only makes sense that we should follow His plan. Doing things His way will lead us to live in harmony with God, with other people and the world we live in. We will never understand everything about our world or why things happen. Some things just do not make sense. But God is in control. By trusting Him and obeying His Word, we can live productive and joyful lives. Living at odds with God's plan only hurts us in the end!!!!! Amen!! Amen!!

Day 174: Relying On God

Think about it: every time we feel frustration, it means we have really stopped relying on God. Frustration hits when we stop depending on Him, and try to make something happen ourselves.

Depending on God for everything may be difficult, but it is the key to the victory we need every single day of our lives.

Choose to stop living independently, and rely on the Holy Spirit. I promise you will not regret it!

126

God, you are all I need. Help me not to trust in myself, but to put my trust in You, and to rely only on You. Amen! Amen!!!!

Day 175: Don't Worry, Stay In Peace, Enjoy God's Blessings

Scriptures says:

Don't worry about anything; instead, pray about everything. Tell God what you need and thank Him for all He has done. Then you will experience God's peace, which exceeds anything we can understand. His peace will guard your hearts and minds as you live in Christ Jesus.

Philippians 4:6-7 NLT

If we genuinely Believe God's Word, then we must apply His Word for God's blessings to truly be effective in our lives.

Truth of the matter is: We spend too much time trying to fix, change, control our situations and/or persons. When things do not go the way we have planned, we result to worldly ways such as drugs, alcohol, sex, etc. THIS ONLY MAKES MATTERS WORSE!!!!!! Do what the Scripture says, be patient and continue meditating on God's Word while you are believing God to act on your behalf.

This Scripture is one of many that tells us exactly what to do to have peace. As you know, if you have true peace then you agree with the Word of God and you can experience all

127

God's blessings, and be a blessing to others so that God receives all the Glory. In Jesus name, Amen!!

Day 176: Speak God's Word To The Mountain

See, we usually talk *about* the "mountains," or challenges, in our lives, but God's Word instructs us to talk *to* them. And when we do, we must respond to them with the Word of God.

We tend to try this for a while, but when we do not see quick results, we stop speaking the Word to our problems, and begin once again to speak to our feelings. Persistence is a vital link to obtaining victory.

Constantly speaking the Word is powerful and necessary in overcoming any problem or negative situation.

Scriptures says:

I tell you the truth, you can say to this mountain, "May you be lifted up and thrown into the sea," and it will happen. But you must really believe it will happen and have no doubt in your heart.

Mark 11:23 NLT

Day 177: Don't Get Robbed Of Your Peace

Where is your Peace, Joy, and Happiness? Get it back. Continue believing and trusting God's Word. God cares and wants us to have His peace.

Scriptures says:

You keep Him in perfect peace whose mind is stayed on you, because He trusts in you. Trust in the Lord forever, for the Lord God is an everlasting rock.

Isaiah 26:3-4

We are robbed of having peace when we feel pressure at work when we look to our job and co-workers for our provision, identity, purpose, and fulfillment. We are robbed of having peace when we feel pressure in our relationships when our worth is not based on God's perspective but the opinions of others. We are robbed of peace when we try and plan our own steps rather than following our God.

My Brothers and Sisters, we must trust God in every area of our lives. Do not settle for pressure, stress, anger, and frustration. Do not settle for sadness and insecurity. Place your trust in God, open your heart, and receive the peace that can only come from our heavenly Father. In Jesus name, Amen!! Amen!!!

Day 178: Being More Like Jesus Is The Way To Peace, Favor, And Victory

Throughout the Bible, God called believers to be faithful to His assignment for them as, well as letting their light shine so all the world could see, no matter how difficult, which included being humble and thinking of others rather than ourselves. Likewise, we must do the same. When we align our lives to God's story, He will allow us to accomplish great things.

Being faithful benefits us as well as the people in our lives. When we are faithful to them, they are blessed as well.

See, Christians are not called to be successful as the world defines success. We are called to be faithful to God in what He calls us to do. We faithfully act in faith toward God and leave the results to Him. In Jesus name, Amen!! Amen!!

Scriptures says:

Don't be selfish; don't try to impress others. Be humble, thinking of others as better than yourselves. Don't look out only for your own interests, but take an interest in others, too.

Philippians 2:3-4 NLT

130

Day 179: God's Way Is Perfect

Scriptures says:

God's way is perfect. All the Lord's promises prove true. He is a shield for all who look to Him for protection.

Psalms 18:30 NLT

Day 180: Continue Believing

Scriptures says:

"If you can?" said Jesus. "Everything is possible for one who believes." Immediately the boy's father exclaimed, "I do believe; help me overcome my unbelief!"

Mark 9:22–24

See, to believe in Jesus and to believe the truths taught in Scriptures will guide our lives daily and into eternity. He does not want you to simply believe these truths are the right answer. He wants you to take them in your heart where they will affect how you will live.

Here is the promise:

What you once thought was impossible will now be possible!! The more you believe, the more you see and discover the power of God!! The more you believe, the more He changes you from the inside out to become the kind of person you have only dreamed about — filled with love, joy, peace, kindness, faithfulness, gentleness and self-control. In Jesus name, Amen!!

Day 181: Facing The Battle

In this life you will have trials and tribulations. Point blank period!!! You are experiencing health related challenges. You are experiencing marital and relationships challenges. You are depressed and miserable. You do not know what God has in store for you. You just cannot seem to figure it out. You are struggling to find a job or the job you have, you are not sure it's for you. You are struggling with your finances. Whatever it may be.

I ask my Brothers and Sisters: What do you do when facing the battle?

Allow me to explain:

Pray and give your situation to God. Believe that it is done. While you are waiting for God to act on your behalf, you should be praising Him, Studying and Meditating on His Word, being a blessing to others, demonstrating true love and spreading His Word. The battle is difficult when you are angered, stressed, and worried, and trying to do things your way. However, when you rest in the finish works of Jesus, then Victory is yours, and just watch God show up and show out in your situation. Amen!! Amen!!

Scriptures says:

Give all your worries and cares to God, for He cares about you.

1 Peter 5:7 NLT

Day 182: Steps To Pursuing God

1. Persistent Prayer Life
2. Study the Word Of God
3. Fully Obey
4. Be Quick to Repent
5. Have A Forgiving Heart
6. Become A Passionate Praiser
7. Honor God with Giving and Service to Others

A lot of times we look to Worldly stuff for pleasure; the dream home, the car, the job, perfect relationships, sex, alcohol, drugs etc.... but these are only temporary pleasure. Something still will be missing because we are pursuing the wrong things. PURSUE GOD!!!!!!!!

God wants us to replace our thoughts, desires and feelings with His. And we cannot live in victory until we do.

Scriptures says:

Joyful are people of integrity, who follow the instructions of the Lord. Joyful are those who obey His laws and search for Him with all their hearts. They do not compromise with evil, and they walk only in His paths.

Psalms 119:1-3 NLT

Day 183: Money: A Blessing Or A Curse?

Scriptures says:

For the love of money is the root of all kinds of evil, and by craving it, some have wandered away from the faith and pierced themselves with many pains.
1 Timothy 6:10 Holman CSB

Our society is in love with money and the things that money can buy. God is not! God cares about people, not possessions, and so must we. We must, to the best of our abilities, love our neighbors as ourselves, and we must, to the best of our abilities, resist the mighty temptation to place possessions ahead of people. Money in and of itself is not evil, but worshipping money is! So today, as you prioritize matters of importance for you and your family, remember that God is almighty, but the dollar is not. If we worship God, we are blessed; but if we worship "the almighty dollar," we are inevitably punished because of our misplaced priorities.

Let us pray:

Dear Lord, I will earn money and I will use money, but I will not worship money. Give me the wisdom and the discipline to be a responsible steward over my financial resources, and let me use those resources for the glory of Your Kingdom. In Jesus name, Amen!

Day 184: Peace And Calmness Is Priceless

Having an attitude of peace and calm is priceless. It is an attitude that says, "I'm trusting God," and it speaks powerfully to people. But it takes time, focus, and the grace of God to be consistently peaceful.

Too often our stress level is tied up in our circumstances. You could be stressed because you are always busy, or you are struggling financially, or because you are not getting along with someone you love.

To conquer the stress in our lives, we need to learn to practice the peace that has been provided for us by the overcoming power of Jesus.

Every day we need to say, "God has given me peace today. I will rejoice and be glad in it."

God, I know that You have overcome any and every obstacle, so I ask You to help me live in the peace that You've provided for me. Show me how to trust You as I live "in the now." Amen!! Amen!!! Thank you, Jesus!!!

Day 185: Worry Is Selfishness In Disguise

Too often, people give in to worry without realizing how deadly it is. When you get to the root of it, worry is a sin. Worry certainly does not come out of faith.

Most of the time, worry is based on one sin in particular: SELFISHNESS. Usually when we worry, we are concerned about how our selfish desires are not being fulfilled. The more selfish desires you have, the more you must worry about, and the more complicated your life becomes.

God wants us to simply focus on serving Him. It is God's will that we live our lives free from all anxiety and distressing care.

Let us pray:

Father God, thank You for showing me that worry is a sin. Help me to get rid of my selfish, ungodly desires so that I can simply pursue Your destiny for me. Amen!!! Amen!!!

Day 186: Want To Receive Your Breakthrough?

First, you need to Pray!!!

Secondly, you need to Believe God for what you are praying for. You only need to ask one time. God hears you the first time. Thirdly, while you are waiting, you need to meditate in God's Word day and night. Speak positive about your situation. This means thanking Him on a day-to-day basis about your situation. Even if it's look like nothing is working, trust me, it is working. Continue to be patient, stay in peace, and watch God work it all out for you. Your BREAKTHROUGH is right around the corner. In Jesus name, Amen!!!

Scriptures says:

I tell you, you can pray for anything, and if you believe that you've received it, it will be yours.

Mark 11:24 NLT

Study this Book of Instruction continually. Meditate on it day and night so you will be sure to obey everything written in it. Only then will you prosper and succeed in all you do.

Joshua 1:8 NLT

Day 187: What Do You Want To Become?

If you're not sure what you're becoming, let me give you a hint: you're going to be whatever you think about and talk about all the time.

So, listen to yourself. If you don't like what you hear, change it. Become better by beginning to think God's Word, talk God's Word, and act on God's Word.

Nobody on Earth can determine what you're going to become but you. Yes, you! Don't blame it on the devil. He can't change it. Don't blame it on your parents, your background, or your circumstances. And certainly don't blame it on God.

You can determine your outcome in life by changing your words to God's Words, and releasing your faith. You can become all you were meant to be.

A man's belly shall be satisfied with the fruit of his mouth; and with the increase of his lips shall he be filled.

Proverbs 18:20 KJV

Day 188: Confession And Believing God's Word

A lot of times we have a hard time calling those things that be not as though they were, but speaking it into existence is demonstrating a form of Faith. No matter what you may be facing and how the situation looks, start speaking positive things and God's Word...

Say with me: "All is well, All is well with my Finances; All is well with my mind; All is well with my body; All is well with my child/children; All is well with my spouse; All is well with whatever's I may be experiencing because All is well with me!! Amen!!"

Abraham beloved God, and God counted him as righteous because of his faith.

Romans 4:3 NLT

Day 189: Receive Your Manifestation

Religion tells us we've got to do something in order to make God move. Ask yourself: "how much do I have to do? I got to Pray more, Fast more, Give more?" NO!! *Believe* more and *Trust* more. Realize God has already moved and lay hold to what Grace has made available.

Ladies and gentlemen God's Grace, Love and Favor has already provided everything we will ever need in this life. Grace is undeserved favor, which means you don't earn it; it is a gift from God. Unbelief is what's stopping manifestation. We must come to a point where we are agreeing what is already done.

It looks like this:

God has already healed me; Faith takes healing so it can be manifested in your life.

God has already prospered me; Faith takes prosperity so it can be manifested in your life.

Scriptures says:

By His divine power God has given us everything we need for living a godly life. We have received all of this by coming to know Him, the one who called us to himself by means of His marvelous glory and excellence.

2 Peter 1:3 NLT

Day 190: Don't Beg, Just Believe

A lot of times we get caught up in wrong religious practice, coming to God when we encounter trials and situations we don't understand.

When we bring our concerns to God, He heard us the FIRST time. We don't need to beg we need to praise Him.

For instance: "Lord please help me; Lord, please heal me and prosper me." NO!!! This is begging. This doesn't move God.

Praising God looks like this: "Thank you for the blessing me, Thank you for healing and prospering me." We must Thank God in Advance even when we don't see instant results. Our Faith is being strengthened as well as claiming the VICTORY in our Trials and Situations!!!!!!!!!!

Day 191: God Causes Things to Happen at the Right Time

Are you waiting for the desires of your heart to begin to manifest? Are you trusting God for prosperity, favor, promotion, honor, and all the blessings found in His Word?

Are you tired of waiting for harvest time in your life? Are you frustrated, crying out, "When, God, when?" Then you need to understand that God's timing is often a mystery. He doesn't do things on our timetable. Yet His Word promises that He will not be late, not one single day.

God causes things to happen at exactly the right time! Your job is not to figure out when, but to make up your mind that you won't give up until you cross the finish line. The more you trust Jesus and keep your eyes focused on Him, the more life you'll have. Trusting God brings life. Believing brings rest. So stop trying to figure everything out, and let God be God in your life. Amen!!

Let us pray:

God, I know that Your timing is perfect, even when I grow tired of waiting. Help me to trust in You and rest in Your plan for me. In Jesus name, Amen!!!

Day 192: The Mess

Let me explain; See, no matter what mess you may be going through, God has already made a way of escape. You don't get to go through something that God won't allow you to win. So whatever mess you may be experiencing right now, I'm telling you: Victory is yours. All you got to do is believe it. You won!!!

Here me out. The mess is preparing you for a greater challenge, once you defeat this mess, the future mess won't look like mess because of the strength you got from the last mess. Go ahead and turn your problems into barbells, and start exercising and building them muscles.

Everything we go through has an expiration date on it. Go ahead and smile, enjoy yourself, it's gonna be alright. Amen!! Amen!!

God blesses those who patiently endure testing and temptation. Afterward they will receive the crown of life God has promised to those who love Him.

James 1:12 NLT

Day 193: It's Turning Around For You

I'm here to encourage you today that whatever you may be experiencing or battling or believing God for. It's turning around for you!!

This is your season for Grace and Favor. This is your season to reap what you have sown.

See, God is making a way. A change is coming. But you got to stand strong and Believe. There is no reason to doubt because God is working it out. Stay in Faith, Stay in your lane, and watch God turn it around for you. In Jesus name, Amen!!!

For I know the plans I have for you, declares the LORD, plans to prosper you and not to harm you, plans to give you hope and a future.

Jeremiah 29:11 NIV

142

Day 194: True Results Come From The Lord

Scriptures says:

Stop at the crossroads and look around. Ask for the old, godly way, and walk in it. Travel its path, and you will find rest for your souls. But you reply, "No, that's not the road we want!"

Jeremiah 6:16 NLT

Think about this Scripture for a moment. See, we want God's blessings to show up in our lives, but we want it how we want it. That's not how God operates. If you want to see the results you are looking for, then search for and stay on the road God has provided for you.

Truth be told, we all want to experience Joy, Happiness, Prosperity and Rest. But in order to truly experience these things on a consistent and lifelong journey, then we must take God's Road!!! In Jesus name, Amen!! Amen!!

Day 195: Second Chance

God has given us chances after chances because of His unfailing love. We ought to do the same to others despite how we have been wronged. When we continue to hold grudges and are unforgiving, our wounds won't heal, and we hinder what God wants to do in our lives. If we're going to be children of God, then let's love like He does.

Bible tells us Adam and Eve got a second chance. Jonah got a second chance; so did Peter. David got a second chance. The children of Israel were given repeated chances. Through Noah, the whole world was given a second chance.

The truth is, we need a second chance because we are all sinners. We all fall short of the mark. We all walk outside the lines. Yet God forgives, restores, and renews when we repent because of His love for us.

He knows that we will fail. He expects that we will stumble, but He also expects that in the process, His children will grow. Let's continue to grow, forgive and demonstrate Godly love and experience all that God has for you and me. In Jesus name, Amen!!!

Day 196: No Need To Worry Or Have Anxious Thoughts

Ok, you may be thinking that's easier said than done. "You're not experiencing the pain that I'm feeling! You're not having financial difficulties like I am! You're not feeling depressed or alone like I am! You're not struggling with marital or relationships issues like I am."

We all experience different challenges in our lives. I can promise you that if you're worrying or stressing then you are not trusting God...

God said: "put me first and all these things shall be added." The Love for God needs to preside over everything in your life. God wants you to give Him all your cares. He is more concerned than you are about what your needs are. He literally wants you to cast all your cares upon Him. This means trusting Him. If you don't, anxiety, worries, and stress places a wall between you and God. This is never good.

Saturate yourself in prayer throughout the day with gratitude each time an anxious thought arises. In Jesus name, Amen!!

Let us pray:

Search me, O God, and know my heart; test me and know my anxious thoughts. Point out anything in me that offends you and lead me along the path of everlasting life. I want to trust You with all my heart, and not depend on my own understanding. As I seek Your will in all I do, You will show me which path to take. May I not worry about anything, but pray about everything. Thank You for all You've done! I Praise You and Bless You! In Jesus name, Amen!!!!!

Day 197: What Brings True Happiness, Peace, And Joy? JESUS!

Money, fame, relationships, and success—these things we chase after— are just temporary satisfaction. Our greatest longing is for Joy, Peace, Happiness, and being Content.

You and I both need something much greater, something stronger and something secure. JESUS!!!! We need HIM!! He's the creator, sustainer, and source of every good thing, and in His presence is "fullness of joy." The more we know Jesus, the more we know joy, peace, and contentment.

Worldly items—the perfect home, a dream job, an amazing vacation, or financial security—may provide momentary happiness but repeatedly fail to satisfy. It's not wrong to enjoy any of these items; but remember where your help comes from.

See, when you just can't seem to figure it out, who's there? Jesus! When finances disappear, who's there? Jesus! When your health has failed you, who's there? Jesus! When it appears that all odds or against you, who's there? Jesus! When your family has turned their back on you, who's there? Jesus! When the enemies are trying to attack, who's there? Jesus! We need Jesus for true joy, peace, happiness and comfort. In Jesus name, Amen!!

Scriptures says:

You will show me the way of life, granting me the joy of your presence and the pleasures of living with you forever.

Psalms 16:11 NLT

Day 198: Strive For Greatness!

There is greatness in you. Your life counts. Your life is important. But if the basis for your self-image comes from the world, you will miss God's vision of you and for you.

Great is knowing that your life counts. Greatness is knowing that someone else's life counts—that someone else's life matters, and not just your own. Great is self-vision, while greatness is God's vision.

Your greatness has nothing to do with external appearance or worldly expectation, but rather living out Kingdom principles that build up other people. Let's continue to strive for greatness. Amen!!! Amen!!!

And he sat down, and called the twelve, and saith unto them, If any man desire to be first, the same shall be last of all, and servant of all.

Mark 9:35 KJV

Day 199: Thank You Lord!

Let us pray:

Dear God, I thank you that you did not give me a spirit of timidity, or cowardice, or craven or cringing or fawning fear. Thank you for giving me a spirit of power, love and calm, and a spirit of well-balanced mind, discipline and self-control. I will put it to good use. Dear God, continue to let Your purpose prevail over the many plans I make. Thank You for causing everything to work together for good because I love You and You call me to Your purpose for my life. When I make my plans, direct my steps. Your Word is a lamp to my feet and a light to my path. You Alone are the Alpha and the Omega, the First and the Last, the Beginning and the End. I give you all the Praise and Glory that you so deserve. THANK YOU, LORD! In Jesus name, Amen!!!

Day 200: Peace And Joy

Always be full of joy in the Lord. I say it again–rejoice! Let everyone see that you are considerate in all you do. Remember, the Lord is coming soon. Don't worry about anything; instead, pray about everything. Tell God what you need and thank Him for all He has done. Then you will experience God's peace, which exceeds anything we can understand. His peace will guard your hearts and minds as you live in Christ Jesus. And now, dear brothers and sisters, one final thing. Fix your thoughts on what is true, and honorable, and right, and pure, and lovely, and admirable. Think about things that are excellent and worthy of praise. Keep putting into practice all you learned and received from me–everything you heard from me and saw me doing. Then the God of peace will be with you.

Philippians 4:4-9 NLT

Follow the Scripture and Don't stop studying God's Word. Abide in God, pray to Him, seek Him continually and experience Peace, Joy and Happiness. Amen!!

Day 201: God Will Provide; Will You Believe It?

We serve a God who abundantly provides for us everything we could ever need. And this is including everything you may be experiencing right now, no matter what it may be. In Jesus name, Amen!!

Scriptures says:

The Lord is my shepherd; I shall not want.

Psalm 23:1

Let those words sink in for a second.

Abundant peace and security is available for you today if you will trust in your heavenly Father's promise to provide everything you need. Trust that He will provide the absolute best life you can live. Whether He provides abundantly in the eyes of the world does not matter.

If you are truly seeking Him and trusting Him with all your heart, you will live the best life possible. He knows what you need. He knows the desires within you. Stop looking to the world for examples of what your life should look like, and seek His will above all else. Look to loving Him and being loved by Him as the best thing in life and all else will fall into place. In Jesus name, Amen!!

Day 202: Cry Out To The Lord

When we think about King David in the Bible, he faced some fearful and challenging situations. But he cried out and depended upon the Lord.

Life can be so hard, so difficult; at times, it can be overwhelming. You might be battling debt, divorce, unemployment, depression, despair, health challenges, a rebellious teenager, addiction, loneliness, discouragement, and more. Likewise, we ought to do what David did and cry out and give our cares to God. He will bring us through!!!!!

- When troubled, worried, or overwhelmed, cry out: "the Lord is my rock."
- When discouraged, cry out: "the Lord is my stronghold."
- When weary, cry out: "the Lord is my strength."

For every need, on every occasion, cry out to God, who is your rock and your refuge, and He will see you through. In Jesus name, Amen!! Amen!!! GIVE YOUR CARES TO GOD!!!

Day 203: Do We Trust In God, Or Do We Trust In Other Things?

We all encounter challenges and burdens, and sometimes these problems feel overwhelming. Unemployment, financial pressure, depression, a rebellious teenager, the death of a loved one, a difficult decision, a feeling of failure, trouble in a marriage, and so much more.

However, when we face these challenges, do we trust in God, or do we trust in other things? Do we trust our own efforts, our own resources, and our own thinking? Do we first look to other people to guide us, rescue us, or protect us? Do we rely on our careful research, our diligent efforts, our network, and our abilities? Is our reliance on the best doctors and wisest counselors?

Now God can use any of these things, of course, and He does. But in our heart of hearts, where is our trust? Where is our confidence? Is our trust in God to guide us and deliver us, or is our trust in ourselves or other people? Wherever it maybe, I encourage and challenge you today to Fully Trust God's Word and experience the Breakthrough you've been waiting on. In Jesus name, Amen!! Amen!!

Day 204: In The Name Of Jesus

No matter what you may be experiencing or going through right now, just call on the name of Jesus and He shall come through!!!!

See, There's Power in the name of Jesus! There's Healing in the name of Jesus! There's Deliverance in the name of Jesus! There's Love in the name of Jesus! There's a Breakthrough in the name of Jesus.

Just call on the name of Jesus, Amen!!! Amen!!!

Day 205: Your Life Won't Change Until Your Thinking Changes

Most of us wake up thinking negative, sad, depressing things about our current situation and problems. This won't cut it if we want to experience God's Victory.

If you struggle with negative thinking, it's important for you to come to grips with the fact that your life won't change until your thinking does. Renewed, God-like thinking is vital for change.

The Bible presents a lot of detailed instruction on what kinds of things we should think about. Philippians 4:8 alone tells us to think about things that build us up, not tear us down.

Instead of waking up in the morning and immediately thinking negative thoughts, try finding positive truth from Scripture and focus on it every day when you wake up. Let God's Word grow in you and transform your mind. Fix your mind on good things and enjoy the godly changes it brings.

Let us pray:

God, I'm ready to change and live with the mind of Christ. Help me to only think about what is true, honorable, pure, lovely, kind, and gracious. In Jesus name, Amen and Amen!!!!!!

Day 206: Cast Your Burdens To God

Scriptures says:

Give your burdens to the Lord, and He will take care of you. He will not permit the godly to slip and fall.
Psalms 55:22 NLT

I'm sure most of us have quoted this Scripture a few times or at least familiar with this Scripture. It's simply says; whatever you may be going through, give it to God. Point blank period! If you are still nursing and rehearsing the problem, or stressing, angered, or worried, THEN YOU "HAVE NOT" GAVE YOUR CARES TO GOD. And the results you are looking for won't be there until you really align yourself with God's Word.

I get it; there are times when the burdens of life are so heavy, so difficult, that it's hard to fully trust that God will work it out. He will! But in His timing, and not ours. Ok. So, what do I do once I give my cares to God? Study Scriptures, meditate day and night on Scriptures, Pray, Listen and Sing Gospel Songs and Praise Him and stay positive...

However, you still might not see immediate results on your situations, but the Holy Ghost will be assisting you with renewing your mind, and your thoughts become positive and not negative, and then in due time, because now you have aligned yourself with God's Word, He will show up and show out on your situation. Amen!! Amen!! In Jesus name, Amen!!!!

Day 207: Give Thanks To The Lord

I give you thanks, O LORD, with all my heart; I will sing your praises before the gods. I bow before your holy Temple as I worship. I praise your name for your unfailing love and faithfulness; for your promises are backed by all the honor of your name. As soon as I pray, you answer me; you encourage me by giving me strength.

Psalms 138:1-3 NLT

Day 208: I Will Praise The Lord At All Times

I will praise the Lord at all times. I will constantly speak His praises.

Psalm 34:1 NLT

It's easy to quote this Scripture especially when all is well, and everything is going just like we have planned it. But will we praise Him when adversity hits, and challenges arise?? Will we put our situations above God? Or will we praise Him and know that He will work it out?

I'm struggling with my finances. I will praise the Lord at all times!! I'm experiencing marital issues. I will praise the Lord at all times!! I feel like I just can't get a break. I will praise the Lord at all times!! I'm experiencing health challenges. I will praise the Lord at all times!!

See, no matter what we may be experiencing or going through we shall praise the Lord at all times. When we do this, we are aligning ourselves with God's Word by demonstrating that no matter what, we are putting our trust into Him instead of our situations. He will work it out as long as we Trust, Believe and Rest in God's Word... In Jesus name, Amen!! Amen!!!

Day 209: Where You Are Weak, He Is Strong

The only way to overcome your weakness is to rely on God's strength. To do that, you have to stop focusing on your weaknesses. You cannot look at everything you are not. You must look at everything God is. Focus on His strength and all He is willing to do for you.

In any area where you stumble, God is ready and willing to provide you with His strength. So the next time you find yourself confronted by your weakness, remember and declare that where you are weak, He is strong!

Let us pray:

God, I declare and confess that where I am weak, You are strong. So, I will not worry about, or remain defeated by, my weakness. Instead, I put my faith in Your strength. Amen!! Amen!!!

Day 210: Oh, Praise Him!

Oftentimes we think about praising God, but because we don't feel like it, we shrug off that prompting in our spirit, and don't do it. But God is worthy of our praise—whether we feel like praising Him or not. We must realize that praise is not governed by our emotions.

Under the old covenant, when the people had problems, they went to the priest and he would offer a sacrifice to God. That would bring God on the scene.

Today, under the new covenant, we are to do the same, only we are the priests under God (Revelation 5:10). As we offer up the sacrifices of praise before our Most High Priest, Jesus, our communication with God is great.

Our praise brings God personally on the scene. At times of high praise, the shekinah glory of God will fill an entire place with His sweet Glory.

So, usher His presence into your situation. Praise Him in the midst of your needs. Praise Him, regardless of your feelings. Obey the Word and praise Him continually. He is worthy to be praised! To praise when you don't feel like it is an act of honor. God said, "He that honors Me, him will I honor."

Scriptures says:

Therefore, let us offer through Jesus a continual sacrifice of praise to God, proclaiming our allegiance to His name.

Hebrews 13:15 NLT

Day 211: Will You Trust The Lord For Real?

Scriptures says:

Trust in the Lord with all your heart; do not depend on your own understanding. Seek His will in all you do, and He will show you which path to take.

Proverbs 3:5-6 NLT

What a promise!!! God will direct us and crown our efforts with success if we put our Trust in Him rather than try to do it on our own. Putting God first means turning our lives and wills over to Him. Surrendering to His lordship is humbling, but He will surely bless us as a result...

Scriptures says:

Seek ye first the Kingdom Of God and His righteousness; and all these things shall be added.

Matthew 6:33

...which means we are not supposed to continue putting our situations and problems first. We must put our trust in God and Believe that He will work it out. Will You Trust The Lord For Real??? Amen!! Amen!!

Day 212: Let It Go!

Scriptures says:

Give all your worries and cares to God, for He cares about you.

1 Peter 5:7 NLT

This Scripture above is considered Bible, which means God's Word. If we are to Believe God's Word, then we must apply His Word to our lives demonstrated by Faith.

Whatever you may be going through right now, just let it go and give it to God. We all experience different challenges in life, and who's to say how one is feeling about their particular situation. I might not feel the way you feel, and you might not feel the way I feel. But if you want to experience Peace, Joy, and Happiness, then you need to let go of your battles and give it God. Then you will experience your breakthrough!! Amen!!! Amen!!

Day 213: Believe God, He Will Stand With Us

Scriptures says:

No one will be able to stand against you as long as you live. For I will be with you as I was with Moses. I will not fail you or abandon you.

Joshua 1:5 NLT

Day 214: God's Word Is Medicine For Victory

Scriptures says:

The Lord is my strength and my song; He has given me the victory.

Psalm 118:14 NLT

The more we continue to learn about God through His Word, we learn of His ways and how we should apply them to our lives. The Bible has left clear guidelines for what we need. However, you must read it!! All we need to do is Trust, Believe and Apply.

Studying, meditating and applying God's Word should become a joyful experience that will fill us with His Word in our hearts and mind and allow us to experience all that He has for us. Amen!! Amen!!!

Day 215: Only You, Lord!

Scriptures says:

You have done many good things for me, Lord, just as you promised. I believe in your commands; now teach me good judgment and knowledge. I used to wander off until you disciplined me; but now I closely follow your Word. You are good and do only good; teach me your decrees.

Psalms 119:65-68 NLT

159

Day 216: You Want To Be Blessed? You Must Trust The Lord

Scriptures says:

But blessed are those who trust in the Lord and have made the Lord their hope and confidence. They are like trees planted along a riverbank, with roots that reach deep into the water. Such trees are not bothered by the heat or worried by long months of drought. Their leaves stay green, and they never stop producing fruit.

Jeremiah 17:7-8 NLT

Day 217: Lord, Lead And Guide Me

Scriptures says:

Search me, O God, and know my heart, test me and know my anxious thoughts. Point out anything in me that offends you and lead me along the path of everlasting life.

Psalms 139:23-24 NLT

Day 218: Who Is Blessed?

Scriptures says:

But blessed are those who trust in the Lord and have made the Lord their hope and confidence.

Jeremiah 17:7 NLT

Day 219: Don't Be So Hard On Yourself!

Many of us at times are too hard on ourselves, saying: "I just can't get it right. Why do I keep making the same mistakes? I just can't shake this addiction, I know I need to get in God's Word," and etc.... Don't Be So Hard On Yourself!!!!

God has a plan for each one of us. All we need to do is allow God's Word to work in our lives. No matter how many mistakes we have made, we can still turn things around with God working within us. It won't happen by our strength alone. We must include God!

Including God means to surrender our lives to Him and seek to follow His will as He reveals it to us. No matter what we have done in the past, God's Grace and His Word will allow restoration and healing among us. Amen!! Amen!!

I–yes, I alone–will blot out your sins for my own sake and will never think of them again.

Isaiah 43:25 NLT

Day 220: The Battle Is Not Yours

Listen, all you people of Judah and Jerusalem! Listen, King Jehoshaphat! This is what the Lord said: Do not be afraid! Don't be discouraged by this mighty army, for the battle is not yours, but God's.

2 Chronicles 20:15 NLT

But you will not even need to fight. Take your positions; then stand still and watch the Lord's victory. He is with you, O people of Judah and Jerusalem. Do not be afraid or discouraged. Go out against them tomorrow, for the Lord is with you!

2 Chronicles 20:17 NLT

Day 221: When Facing Adversity

Scriptures says:

When you go through deep waters, I will be with you.

When you go through rivers of difficulty, you will not drown.

When you walk through the fire of oppression, you will not be burned up; the flames will not consume you.

Isaiah 43:2 NLT

Day 222: Follow God, Let Him Lead

Scriptures says:

Trust in the Lord with all your heart, do not depend on your own understanding. Seek His will in all you do, and He will show you which path to take.

Proverbs 3:5-6 NLT

Day 223: Trouble and Worries Won't Last, God's Word Will

Scriptures says:

Don't worry about anything; instead, pray about everything. Tell God what you need and thank Him for all He has done. Then you will experience God's peace, which exceeds anything we can understand. His peace will guard your hearts and minds as you live in Christ Jesus.

Philippians 4:6-7 NLT

Day 224: Listen! Get The Word Of God On Your Situation!

Are You Troubled??

Scriptures says:

Don't let your hearts be troubled. Trust in God, and trust also in me.

John 14:1 NLT

Are You Struggling Financially?

And this same God who takes care of me will supply all your needs from His glorious riches, which have been given to us in Christ Jesus.

Philippians 4:19 NLT

Growing Weary??

164

Then Jesus said, "Come to me, all of you who are weary and carry heavy burdens, and I will give you rest."

Matthew 11:28 NLT

Seeking Provision??

"For I know the plans I haves for you," says the Lord. "They are plans for good and not for disaster, to give you a future and a hope."

Jeremiah 29:11 NLT

"GET THE WORD ON IT" Amen!! Amen!!!

Day 225: Remain With The Lord

Scriptures says:

Yes, I am the vine; you are the branches. Those who remain in me, and I in them, will produce much fruit. For apart from me you can do nothing.

John 15:5 NLT

Day 226: Give God First Priority In Your Life. Guess What's Next?

Scriptures says:

Seek the Kingdom of God above all else, and live righteously, and He will give you everything you need.

Matthew 6:33 NLT

Day 227: You Can Do It, Don't Give Up!

Scriptures says:

For I can do everything through Christ, who gives me strength.

Philippians 4:13 NLT

Day 228: Slow Down, Wait, Allow God To Lead

Scriptures says:

Even the youths shall faint and be weary, and the young men shall utterly fall: But they that wait upon the Lord shall renew their strength; they shall mount up with wings as eagles; they shall run, and not be weary; and they shall walk, and not faint.

Isaiah 40:30-31 KJV

Day 229: We Have The Victory!

Let us pray:

Lord, this is the day that you have made, and we shall rejoice and be glad in it. Satan is under our feet. We are not

166

moved by adversity and trying situations. We have been made the righteousness of God in Christ Jesus. We dwell in the Kingdom of God and have peace and joy in the Holy Spirit! We thank you right now in advance for Victory!! In Jesus name we pray, Amen!! Amen!!

Day 230: Do It God's Way; Just Submit

Scriptures says:

Submit to God, and you will have peace; then things will go well for you. Listen to His instructions and store them in your heart.

Job 22:21-22 NLT

Day 231: Don't Worry 'Bout Your Haters; Continue Walking With God

Scriptures says:

When a man's ways please the Lord, He maketh even his enemies to be at peace with him.

Proverbs 16:7 KJV

Day 232: Let's Build Up Each Other Daily

Scriptures says:

So then let us aim for harmony in the church and try to build up each other up.

Romans 14:19 NLT

Day 233: No Matter What

Scriptures says:

Be thankful in all circumstances, for this is God's will for you who belong to Christ Jesus.

1 Thessalonians 5:18 NLT

Day 234: All You Need

Scriptures says:

Each time he said, "My grace is all you need. My power works best in weakness." So now I am glad to boast about my weaknesses, so that the power of Christ can work through me.

2 Corinthians 12:9 NLT

Day 235: God Will Supply

Scriptures says:

But my God shall supply all your need according to His riches in glory by Christ Jesus.

Philippians 4:19 KJV

Day 236: Be Strong!

Scriptures says:

This is my command- be strong and courageous! Do not be afraid or discouraged. For the Lord God is with you wherever you go.

Joshua 1:9 NLT

Day 237: The Gift From God

Just a reminder, everything we have comes from almighty God. A lot of times we caught up in worldly things. Such things like our achievements, possession, money, job, talents, skills set etc… Well, all of this might be true, but we must never forget where it all came from. The Gift From God.

What do you have that God hasn't given you? And if everything you have is from God, why boast as though it were not a gift?

1 Corinthians 4:7 NLT

Day 238: Keep Your Mind On Jesus, He Will Work It Out

Man, what a powerful true statement… See, in order to endure whatever we may be experiencing, we must keep our mind on Jesus. We must meditate on His Word day and night. I'm not talking about just memorizing Scriptures, which is fine. Listen, quoting Scriptures won't feed you. You have to do more like studying, meditating, believe and live the Word out to be spiritually fed. This allow us to keep our mind on Jesus.

When everything you have tried fails. Keep your mind on Jesus! You get a negative report from the doctor. Keep your mind on Jesus! Are you experiencing financial challenges? Keep your mind on Jesus! Having marital issues? Keep your mind on Jesus! Trying to break an addiction? Keep your mind on Jesus! Just don't know what to do about it all. Keep your mind on Jesus and all will work out for your good. In Jesus name, Amen! Amen!!!

We are pressed on every side by troubles, but we are not crushed. We are perplexed, but not driven to despair. We are hunted down, but never abandoned by God. We get knocked down, but we are not destroyed.

2 Corinthians 4:8-9 NLT

Day 239: Don't Worry About Your Haters, Backstabbers, Or Those Who Rise Against You

Scriptures says:

Day by day the Lord takes care of the innocent, and they will receive an inheritance that lasts forever. They will not be disgraced in hard times; even in famine they will have more than enough.

Psalms 37:18-19 NLT

Day 240: I Know It's Hard, Just Keep Believing

Jesus said unto him, "If thou canst believe, all things are possible to him that believeth."

And straightway the father of the child cried out, and said with tears, "Lord, I believe; help thou mine unbelief."

Mark 9:23-24 KJV

Truth of the matter is we all have come to that point in our lives where we were believing but our circumstances allowed us to drift into unbelief and doubting Gods words.

The devil is busy and trying to knock us off our faith walk. We must stand strong and stay in God's Word to continue to strengthen our faith journey.

Victory is ours when we continue to believe God's Word. What you're worried or stressed about, God has already worked it out. In Jesus name, Amen!! Amen!!

Day 241: Eternal Rescuer

God is a good God; He will rescue us from any situation or circumstances that we may have if we allow Him to work in our lives and agree with what the Word of God says. One may ask, "how does God rescue us?"

- He swoops you up like an eagle to get you to where He would have you
- He's right there with you running with you while you go through your storm
- He doesn't change the situation, but He changes you and you begin to see the situation differently.

Scriptures says:

And the Lord will deliver me from every evil work and preserve me for His heavenly kingdom. To Him be glory forever and ever. Amen!

2 Timothy 4:18 NKJV

Day 242: God Can Deliver

In times of crises, it's easy to feel like God can't deliver. But God always delivers. We have to change our mindset and cooperate with the Word of God. This way we will understand the true deliverance of God in any situation.

God can deliver His children out of any circumstance. Know today that His power to deliver is bigger than your problem.

Let us pray:

God, time and time again, You have delivered Your children from trouble, and I know You won't fail now. You are more than able to deal with my situation, so I trust in You. In Jesus name I pray, Amen!!! Amen!!!!!!

Day 243: The Lord Is Good

Scriptures says:

The Lord is good, a strong refuge when trouble comes. He is close to those who trust in Him.

Nahum 1:7 NLT

Day 244: Don't Be Premature

Let me explain:

Wait!! Consult with God first. The Bible says seek the Kingdom and His righteousness and all these things shall be added.

A lot of times we miss our blessings because we're tired of waiting on God, and when we get tired of waiting, we will try to manufacture what we don't have. "If you make a blessing, you will miss your blessings." Let this simmer... This can be real trouble. We feel like we need to help God. We must be patient and let God be God... Start communicating with God. This way you will have heard from God. Then obey and Trust God. Wait for time; time reveals all things. In Jesus name, Amen and Amen!!!!!

Scriptures says:

But let patience have her perfect work, that ye may be perfect and entire, wanting nothing.

James 1:4 KJV

174

Day 245: Get Out The Way!

Don't create the season, then complain about the weather!!!!!

Scriptures says:

He must increase, but I must decrease.

John 3:30 NASB

Day 246: Stand Tall

Scriptures says:

Be on guard. Stand firm in the faith. Be courageous. Be strong.

1 Corinthians 16:13 NLT

I prayed to the Lord, and He answered me. He freed me from all my fears.

Psalms 34:4 NLT

Let us pray:

Jesus, teach us how to stand firm. Help us to be faithful to you. Fill us with power and whatever it takes to make it through our trials and tribulations. We thank you for Victory as we follow your ways. In Jesus' Name, Amen and Amen!!!!

Day 247: Be Mindful; Everything Comes From God

My brothers and sisters, we need to remember that our help comes from the Lord. Everything we have comes from the Lord such as your body, your health, your home, your career, your finances, and etc....

We can't allow ourselves to get caught up with stuff and forget the ONE who allowed us to have the stuff. Let's continue to praise God each and every day and give Him first Priority rather than putting our earthly possessions first. Amen!!

Scriptures says:

O Israel, stay away from idols! I am the one who answers your prayers and cares for you. I am like a tree that is always green; all your fruit comes from me.

Hosea 14:8 NLT

Day 248: Something Is About To Happen

Something is about to happen in Your Soul, Your Health, Your Finances, Your Marriage, Your Relationship, Your Spirit, Your Family, and Your Career.

However, in order for something to happen, you must stop rehearsing the old and get on with the new. Bible tells us to

176

forget about the past and look forward to what lies ahead by pressing on. It takes Faith for this to work. Either you gonna Trust Him or you ain't! Either you gonna Believe Him or you ain't. Do you want something to happen??? Believe it!!! Something is about to happen. In Jesus name, Amen!!!!

Scriptures says:

No, dear brothers and sisters, I have not achieved it, but I focus on this one thing: Forgetting the past and looking forward to what lies ahead, I press on to reach the end of the race and receive the heavenly prize for which God, through Christ Jesus, is calling us.

Philippians 3:13-14 NLT

Day 249: Let Him Do It; He Will Guide And Provide

Have you ever been in a place and wonder, "what is going on, where are you Lord, I need you, what do you want me to do Lord?" You might be in this very place right now... No matter the battles you may be facing, just give it God and you remain in peace. Stop stressing. Don't Worry!!!

Get in God's Word, Trust Him, Believe Him and the outcome shall be Victorious!!!! In Jesus name, Amen!!!

The Lord will guide you always;

He will satisfy your needs in a sun-scorched land

and will strengthen your frame.

You will be like a well-watered garden,

like a spring whose waters never fail.

Isaiah 58:11 NIV

Day 250: Just Wait On The Lord

See, you probably saying, "Wait? How much longer do I have to wait? I've been waiting. I'm getting weary. Where are you Lord? I've been praying, studying, and believing. How much longer?" My Brothers and Sisters, I'm here to let you know that the Lord has not forgotten you. Just continue to wait. He will see you through.

Whatever you may be experiencing right now; Wait on the Lord! You may be experiencing financial difficulties. Wait on the Lord! You and your spouse may be having marital issues. Wait on the Lord! You need a breakthrough. Wait on the Lord! You need healing. Wait on the Lord. I encourage you today, whatever you have been praying to God for, just continue to Wait!!!

While you wait, continue to Pray, Study God's Word, Be a Blessing to others, Believe God's Word, and remain in Peace. Amen!! Amen!!

Wait patiently for the Lord. Be brave and courageous. Yes, wait patiently for the Lord.

Psalms 27:14 NLT

Day 251: Why Is It So Hard To Trust God?

Fear!!

Fear holds us back from trusting and believing. Fear paralyzes. Fear makes our painful memories much more intense. Fear breeds despair about the future and makes us not like our present very much either. Fear makes us blind to the blessings we have, and fear makes it difficult, even impossible, to believe that there will be good things to come.

When you find yourself being afraid, take a deep breath, listen to these words of God, and remember that you are being cradled in God's excessively big hands. You are safe. You will prosper. You will be strengthened.

Scriptures says:

So do not fear, for I am with you; do not be dismayed, for I am your God. I will strengthen you and help you; I will uphold you with my righteous right hand.

Isaiah 41:10

In Jesus name, Amen!!!

Day 252: Give Up Your Cares And Worries

I know it's hard to do at times, based upon your situation and circumstances. However, when we are worried and stressed then we are putting our situations over God and we are not trusting Him. We WON'T see manifestation like this.

See, God wants to take care of us. But He wants us to give all our cares, problems, and failures to Him. When we do this, we are displaying trust.

Many of us want God to take care of our situations quick, fast and in a hurry, but we continue worrying or trying to figure out the answers of our problems instead of waiting for God's direction. But it doesn't work that way, God can only do a mighty work with us when we give it all to Him. So, give up your worries and concerns to Him and enjoy His protection, stability, and fullness of joy. In Jesus name, Amen and Amen!!!

Scriptures says:

Give all your worries and cares to God, for He cares about you.

1 Peter 5:7 NLT

Day 253: Stop Worrying

Worrying does us absolutely no good. All it does is make a situation worse with disease, pain and discomfort. It doesn't change one thing, and we waste time by being upset over stuff we can't do anything about, things only God can change. Just put it in the rear and move forward.

The Bible says we can't even add one inch to our height by worrying. Yet, we worry, worry, worry, which gets us nowhere. I mean NOWHERE....

Every time we get really upset, it takes a lot of emotional energy, tires us out, messes with our health, steals our joy, and still doesn't change one thing. We need to stop trying to fix things that only God can fix.

Let us pray:

Lord, my worrying really doesn't accomplish anything, so I leave it behind. I'm so thankful that You can fix what I can't. You calm me down and cheer me up! In Jesus name, Amen!!!!!

Day 254: Facing Difficulties In Life

We all face difficult times. As we struggle with the storms and difficulties of life, our strength often drains to its lowest point. Maybe you're feeling this way right now!! I want to encourage you that during these times of weakness we must look to our God for strength.

181

Then Jesus said, "Come to me, all of you who are weary and carry heavy burdens, and I will give you rest."

Matthew 11:28

Ok. If we Believe God's Word, then we must do what it says:

Give all your worries and cares to God, for He cares about you.

1 Peter 5:7

My brothers and sisters, we must get and stay in the Word of God to experience Peace during our difficulties of life. Check this; if we continue to drag around in defeat, holding our heads down, stressed and worried, then we are only making matters worse. I encourage you today to continue to TRUST and LEAN on GODS WORD FOR REAL!!!! In Jesus name, Amen!! Amen!!

Day 255: Do You Believe?

They told him, "We have seen the Lord!" But he replied, "I won't believe it unless I see the nail wounds in His hands, put my fingers into them, and place my hand into the wound in His side." Eight days later the disciples were together again, and this time Thomas was with them. The doors were locked; but suddenly, as before, Jesus was standing among them. "Peace be with you," he said. Then he said to Thomas, "Put your finger here, and look at my hands. Put your hand into the wound in my side. Don't be faithless any longer. Believe!" "My Lord and my God!" Thomas exclaimed. Then Jesus told him, "You believe because you have seen me. Blessed are those who believe without seeing me."

John 20:25-29 NLT

See, Scriptures says: "blessed are those who believe without seeing." This demonstrates true Faith in God.

We have to come to a point where we believe God's Word no matter how the situation looks in the natural. Because once we demonstrate Faith by continuing to stay in God's Word and Praising Him, manifestation will show up because now we agree with God's Word. Amen!!! Amen!!

Day 256: Doing It The Bible Way

Scriptures says:

I will bless the Lord at ALL times, His praises shall continually be in my mouth.

Psalm 34

My marriage might not be going the way I want it, I will bless the Lord at all times! My finances aren't adding up, I will bless the Lord at all times! I'm experiencing health challenges, I will bless the Lord at all times! I feel so alone, I will bless the Lord at all times.

You might ask "Why?" In Matthew 6:33 it says: seek first His Kingdom and His Righteousness and all these things will be added (prosperity, peace, joy, happiness, healing and etc.).

You might ask "How?" In Philippians 4:13 it says: I can do all things through Christ which strengthens me.

Continue to Pray, Study, Meditate, Give Thanks and Praises, and Believe God's Word. This is doing it the Bible way and you shall overcome all that you may be experiencing. In Jesus name, Amen!!! Amen!!

Day 257: Why Change?

See, when we choose to surrender our lives to God and commit ourselves to His will, we begin to enter into an intimate relationship with God which ultimately brings true joy and happiness.

Making good changes in our lives won't make everyone happy. Some will wonder why you changed, or why you don't relate with peers and family members like you did in the past. Some will even criticize us while we are going through the process or feel like we may be acting funny. But God knows the heart and He will always be with us.

With God's help we will find strength to press on in the next chapter of our lives by doing it God's way and experiencing His righteousness, Grace, Mercy, Joy, Peace and prosperity which the World can't give. This is why Change is Good. In Jesus name, Amen and Amen!!!

Scriptures says:

Don't copy the behavior and customs of this world, but let God transform you into a new person by changing the way you think. Then you will learn to know God's will for you, which is good and pleasing and perfect.

Romans 12:2 NLT

Day 258: The Puzzles Of Life Will Come Together

Have you ever took a thousand-piece puzzle and dumped it all on the table? There's a picture on the box of what the puzzle should look like. However, the pieces on the table looks like a total mess, and it's looks discouraging:

1. While I'm in financial distress; it doesn't look like the picture.
2. I've just been terminated from a job; it doesn't look like the picture.
3. My health is being attacked; it doesn't look like the picture.
4. While I'm in foreclosure and losing my dream home; it doesn't look like the picture.
5. Nothing seems to be making sense; it doesn't look like the picture.
6. I've been searching for a mate; it doesn't look like the picture.
7. My marriage is headed for divorce; it doesn't look like the picture.

I'm here to let you know: keep praising Him, keep serving Him, Keep believing and trusting Him. That picture will eventually come together.

Scriptures says:

And we know that God causes ALL things to work together, for the good of those who love God and are called ACCORDING to HIS purpose for them.

Romans 8:28 NLT

Day 259: How Much Faith Do You Have?

Everything we could ever need is waiting for us in the realm of the spirit with our name on it. It's called FAITH!!!!!!

Faith is the substance of things hoped for, the evidence of things not seen.

Hebrews 11:1

The problem is, many of us don't have a clue about faith, where faith actually comes from, where it's stored or how to get it out when we need it. That's crucial information.

Where does faith come from? Romans 10:17 says: Faith cometh by hearing, and hearing by the Word of God.

This mean we have to study the Word of God; reading the Bible, attending church and etc.…

Where is faith stored? Your faith is stored up in your heart—and since your faith (or lack of it) determines your future, the truth is, your future is stored up in your heart as well.

Don't talk to your situations or circumstances. Don't "tell it the way it is" (or looks, in other words). Speak the end result. Say what God says the outcome is going to be. Faith calls things as though they were.

Let me ask you this: How much faith do you have in your heart right now? Is it enough to handle your current situation? Is it enough to produce victory every day of your

186

life? If not, you'd better start making some big deposits of God's Word. Amen!! And Amen!!!!!

Day 260: The Word Is Truth

Truth goes beyond facts. The fact may be that you don't have any money. The fact may be that the doctor said you have an incurable disease. But what does the truth have to say about it?

You see, the truth is absolute. Truth doesn't yield. Truth doesn't change. Thus, facts are subject to truth.

It can be a fact that you are sick as can be, but God says you were healed by the stripes of Jesus when He died on the cross. That's the truth. Now you have a choice. You can apply the truth of God's Word to the fact that you're sick, and the fact will change—or you can agree with the facts, and things will stay like they are.

I'll tell you right now, God's Word will be quiet—until it starts coming out of your mouth.

But once that Word begins to come out of your mouth in faith, it will be the final Word. If it's God's Word about healing, you'll be healed. If it's His Word about prosperity, you'll be prosperous. If it's His Word about deliverance, you'll be delivered.

When you do your part by believing, speaking and acting on a heart full of faith, God's Word will come to pass.

So, forget all those stories you have heard about so-and-so who believed the Word and it didn't work for them. Truth be told if you genuinely believe and apply it correctly it works.

Sanctify them by Your truth. Your Word is truth.
John 17:17 NKJV

Day 261: Hold On! It's Coming!

See, many of us have been believing God for a while and are wondering, "when will my breakthrough show up? Day by day, month by month and year by year, and it still hasn't showed up." I'm here to encourage you today to Hold On, It's Coming!!

Scriptures says:

So do not throw away this confident trust in the Lord. Remember the great reward it bring you! PATIENT ENDURANCE is what you need now, so that you will continue to do God's Will. Then you will receive all that He has promised.
Hebrews 10:35-36

See, in the midst of waiting we need to develop that childlike faith. Once a child is told something, they go around day after day talking about what they're getting before it shows up. We need to exercise this same type of faith as well. Continue to have confidence in the giver (Lord) of the gift. Continue to speak whatever it is you're believing God for into existence until it's shows up.

Just stay in God's Word, Stay in Faith, Stay in a posture of Praise, Meditate on His Word. This allow us to agree with God's Word to receive our manifestation. Just Hold on, It's coming. In Jesus name, Amen and Amen!!!!!!

Day 262: Supporting Each Other

It's a real good thing when Christians and Believers support one another during our spiritual journey. Often times, when we are going through the process to develop our faith, it might be a little rough, we might not look like a new creation in Christ yet, or we need others to lean on for questions, answers, guidance, and etc.

Let's be mindful to continue to demonstrate true love to others and always ask ourselves: "What would Jesus do? How would Jesus behave?" We must continue to lift ourselves and others up, and never condemn or put Believers or Unbelievers down. Let's Equip and Encourage!! In Jesus name, Amen!! Amen!!

Scriptures says:

I pray that your love will overflow more and more, and that you will keep on growing in knowledge and understanding. For I want you to understand what really matters, so that you may live pure and blameless lives until the day of Christ's return.

Philippians 1:9-10 NLT

Day 263: Speak To Your Situation

The Bible tells us in Genesis, located in the beginning of verses 3, 6, 9, 11, 14, 20, 24, 26, and 29: "And God said." Then at the very end of Genesis 31 its states: "And God saw!!!"

See, God spoke to the situation. He saw come to pass what He said. Likewise, we must demonstrate the same type of belief by speaking positive light to our situations and circumstances until we see it come to pass.

A lot of times we find ourselves putting our situation over God, begin to doubt, speaking negative to our situations and circumstances. We won't see Manifestation like this!!! We must continue to put God First over our situations, remain positive and speak what the Word of God says. Then we shall be victorious. In Jesus name, Amen and Amen!!!!

Day 264: Don't Faint, Don't Get Weary

Your breakthrough and blessings that you have been believing God for is around the corner. I know it's been hard. I know it's been difficult. Trust God that everything will work out.

Learn to live today for today. Even though situations and circumstances might not be going the way you want, be thankful for Today…. The Bible tells us when we always give thanks, He will cause us to triumph. Everything will work out in due time. Don't faint, Don't get weary… In Jesus name, Amen and Amen!!!

Scriptures says:

And let us not be weary in well doing for in due season we shall reap, if we faint not.

Galatians 6:9 KJV

Day 265: Steps For Manifestation

1. **Seek The Kingdom First.** The Bible says seek the Kingdom first and His righteousnesss, and all these things shall be added.
2. **Focus.** Stay focused on God at all times no matter your circumstances.
3. **Develop A Faith Of Confession.** Speak and believe what you want to see manifest in your life.
4. **Know Your Value.** If you don't know your worth, nobody else will either.
5. **Carefully Build And Shape Your Circle Of Influences.** Watch the company you keep. It might be time to get rid of the old and on with new…

I genuinely believe that if you apply these steps, you will and shall see Manifestation, Breakthrough, Joy, Peace and Happiness. In Jesus name, Amen!!

Day 266: Truly Believing Will Produce Blessings And Miracles

Scriptures says:

A woman in the crowd had suffered for twelve years with constant bleeding. She had suffered a great deal from many doctors, and over the years she had

191

spent everything she had to pay them, but she had gotten no better. In fact, she had gotten worse. She had heard about Jesus, so she came up behind Him through the crowd and touched His robe. For she thought to herself, "If I can just touch His robe, I will be healed." Immediately the bleeding stopped, and she could feel in her body that she had been healed of her terrible condition.

Mark 5:25-29 NLT

Wow!!! How powerful is this. She heard about Jesus and believe what he could do, and she was instantly healed. Ladies and gentlemen, this is the blueprint. This works for us as well. We must trust and believe no matter what our situation is or how it's look. Now we can't touch Jesus in the physical realm, but we have the Word of God. Amen!!! Amen!!!

Hold on!!! Jesus then told her, "Daughter your Faith has made you well. Go in peace. Your suffering is over." So, you see what's the results are when you Truly Believe The Word Of GOD!!!! Amen!!!

Day 267: Keep Your Head Up, Don't Get Fed Up

Even though we are pursuing spiritual growth, there will be times when we get discouraged. When we do, it's is important to remember all that God has done for us and to recall the times in the past when God help was present; this is part of seeing the truth.

We also need to remind ourselves of God's promises for the future; this is also part of seeing the truth. When we view our present Distress in the light of God's past Faithfulness and Promises for the future, this encourages us to redirect the course of our lives towards the life God has for us.

Scriptures says:

Teach me to do your will, for you are my God. May your gracious Spirit lead me forward on a firm footing. For the glory of your name, O Lord, preserve my life. Because of your faithfulness, bring me out of this distress.

Psalm 143:10-11 NLT

Day 268: Staying With God

The pain, difficulties, and harsh realities are just part of life in which we live in. Staying with God allows us to handle what is presented before us. When our eyes are on Christ, we begin to see our situations and circumstances from a different perspective.

See, there is hope, even when it's seems like everything is going wrong. When God is at the center of it all, we see things from an eternal perspective, the struggles of life don't disappear; rather we begin to see God's love, Power, and His promises at work on our behalf.

As we continue Staying with God, no obstacles is too great for us to overcome. We shall prevail and victory is ours in Christ Jesus. Amen!! Amen!!

Day 269: Anyone Worried? Stop!

If you're Worrying or Fretting about something, then you are not Trusting GOD. The longer you Focus on the problem, the larger it becomes. Focus On GOD!!!!!!

Scriptures says:

Give your burdens to the LORD, and He will take care of you. He will not permit the godly to slip and fall.

Psalms 55:22 NLT

Day 270: Be The Best You Can Be

Dear brothers and sisters, let's continue to Stay in God's Word, Demonstrate True Love to others, Spread the Good News, and Pray daily.

When difficult situations arises at times, we sometimes lose our Hope and Faith and resort back to our old ways. Let's all continue to be encouraged with what the Word of God says to overcome our daily life struggles. Just be the best we can be!!!!!!

Scriptures says:

I'm not saying that I have this all together, that I have it made. But I am well on my way, reaching out for Christ, who has so wondrously reached out for me. Friends don't get me wrong: By no means do I count myself an expert in all of this, but I've got my eye on the goal, where God is beckoning us onward–to Jesus. I'm off and running, and I'm not turning back.

Philippians 3:12-14 MSG

Day 271: Why Do We Ask "Why?"

Do you ever find yourself in a tragic situation and asked God, "Why? Why is this happening to me?"

For one moment, let's imagine that God actually answered that question. Would His explanation change anything? The effects of the tragedy would still be with you, and the pain would be just as severe as it was before. What would you have learned?

When we ask God that question, I think the real questions we're asking are: "God, do You love me? Will You take care of me in my sorrow and pain? You won't leave me alone, will You?" Is it possible that, because we're afraid God doesn't genuinely care about us, we ask for explanations?

Instead, we must learn to say: "Lord, I believe. I don't understand, and I'll probably never grasp all the reasons bad things happen, but I know for certain that You love me and are with me, always."

I believe it often takes more faith to go through something victoriously than to be delivered from it. Put your faith in God and you'll come out stronger on the other side.

Let us pray:

God, I believe in You, even when circumstances try to fill my mind with doubt. Help me to remember Your love for me and to put my faith in You, no matter what happens.

195

Day 272: It's Never As Hard As It Looks

When hard times come, they're never as hard as they look. That's important. Hard times are not as hard as they look— unless you are looking in the wrong place, through the wrong eyes, thinking the wrong thoughts, and imitating the wrong people.

Some problems look absolutely hopeless and insurmountable. But with a little changing of your thinking, they're not as big of a problem as you thought.

You see, wrong thoughts will paint the wrong pictures in your mind. They'll tell you things are worse than they are. They'll tell you that you don't have what it takes to succeed in life, or that the right opportunity won't come to you.

So the answer to every problem is in the Word. Let God's Word change your thinking. Remember, times are not as hard as they look when you look from God's viewpoint! Amen!! Amen!!

Scriptures says:

"My thoughts are nothing like your thoughts," says the Lord. "And my ways are far beyond anything you could imagine. For just as the heavens are higher than the earth, so my ways are higher than your ways and my thoughts higher than your thoughts.

Isaiah 55:8-9 NLT

Day 273: Get This In Your Spirit

God is about to do something amazing in your life. God is about to take you where you could not go on your own, God is about to show you favor that you could never imagine. Get ready!!

Maybe you have struggled with your finances for a while, maybe you have struggled with an addiction for a while, maybe you feel like life is just not treating you well or maybe you have been dealing with a sickness for a while. Whatever it may be, God is about to show you abundance like you never seen before, He's about to show you peace like you never seen before, He's about to show you joy like you never seen before. God is about to take you to higher heights with confidence and boldness.

Now all you have to do is say: "YES LORD THIS IS FOR ME AND I RECIVE THIS IN MY SPIRIT."

Scriptures says:

The Lord replied, "Listen, I am making a covenant with you in the presence of all your people. I will perform miracles that have never been performed anywhere in the nation. And all the people around you will see the power of the LORD-the awesome power I will display for you."

Exodus 34:10 NLT

Day 274: Walking With A Whole Heart

Second Chronicles 6:14 says: "God shows mercy to those who walk before Him with all their hearts." So, if you're in trouble today, take an honest look at your relationship with God.

Ask yourself, "Am I walking before God with all my heart?"

Let me tell you why that's important. It's not that God is holding out on you and begrudging you His deliverance when you aren't living before Him wholeheartedly like you know you should. But your personal faith level is affected. You are not believing God's Word like you should.

So check your heart today. If you're following Him with your whole heart, there's a great and mighty confidence that comes up within you. No devil can shake that confidence. No matter what happens, you remain certain that God will deliver you!

Scriptures says:

He prayed, "O Lord, God of Israel, there is no God like you in all of heaven and earth. You keep your covenant and show unfailing love to all who walk before you in wholehearted devotion."

2 Chronicles 6:14 NLT

Day 275: If We Reject Jesus, There's No Way Out

See, many of us wants to change for the better, or see different results in our lives. Here the issues: we can't do it alone no matter how hard we try. We need God's Word and the Holy Spirit to assist us.

If we don't BELIEVE God's Word, then we simply are rejecting what Jesus has done on the cross and there will be no way out of our mess, because we have rejected the only way out, which is Jesus. There's no way out of the brokenness you're in! There's no way out of the addiction! There's no way out of the stress, heartache, and pain!

Here's the issue: we think by our own self-efforts we can fix our problems. We can't! We might experience temporary relief for a while, but eventually the issues are right back again. We need Jesus in order for deliverance. Amen! Amen!!

Scriptures says:

I have come as a light to shine in this dark world, so that all who put their trust in me will no longer remain in the dark.

John 12:46 NLT

Day 276: Don't Contradict The Promises Of God

See, when focus more on our situations and circumstances, it's hard to see and believe the promises of God. We need to focus more on God's Word (The Promise) than our situations and circumstances.

My brothers and sisters, it all starts with our THINKING. Majority of the time the reason why we don't see our manifestation is because we don't allow ourselves to agree with God's Word.

For example, the Bible tells us in Isaiah 53:5: "And by His stripes we are healed." But the doctor tells you that you have a health challenge. Here's the issue, we focus more on what the doctor said than what God's Word says. Wrong Thinking!!!

We must not let our situations and circumstances become bigger than God's Word, which are the promises.

Scriptures says:

Study this Book of Instruction continually. Meditate on it day and night so you will be sure to obey everything written in it. Only then will you prosper and succeed in all you do.

Joshua 1:8

So you see, if we do this then we won't be in contradiction with the promises of God. In Jesus name, Amen and Amen!!!!!!!

200

Day 277: Get Ready!

God is about to do some new and amazing things in your life. As of matter of fact, He's already began. Healing is moving throughout your body. You're being delivered right now. Marriages are being restored. Families are being restored. Financial increase is available. Addictions are being broken. Whatever you have been believing God for. GET READY!!! It's about to be an overflow... Just keep your eyes on Jesus and Watch. Amen!! Amen!!

Scriptures says:

For I am about to do something new. See, I have already begun! Do you not see it? I will make a pathway through the wilderness. I will create rivers in the dry wasteland.

Isaiah 43:19 NLT

Day 278: Believe It, Receive It!

Let us pray:

Jesus, you are the Son of God, and I will praise your name forever and never stop trusting you. You are my High Priest, and you understand my weakness. You search hearts and know the mind of the Spirit, because you intercede for the saints according to God will. Whatever I ask for in prayer, I believe that it is granted to me and I will receive it. Thank you, Holy Spirit, for directing me, giving me a clean heart and renewing of my mind. I believe it and receive it. Therefore, I ask whatever I will, and it shall be done for me. In Jesus name I pray, Amen and Amen!!!!!!!

Day 279: The Plans

See, a lot of times in this world, we want to do what we want to do and expect the results to go in our favor. It doesn't work this way, especially long-term.

If we want to experience long-term blessings of the Lord, then we need to choose to do things God's way which is good, pleasing and perfect. Just ponder on this Scripture for a minute:

Scriptures says:

"For I know the plans I have for you," says the Lord. "They are plans for good and not for disaster, to give you a future and a hope."

Jeremiah 29:11 NLT

You see what I'm saying now!! The Lord's plan is always the way to go. Do it His way and not your way. In Jesus name, Amen! Amen!

Day 280: Listen And Follow God's Word

Anyone who listens to my teaching and follows it is wise, like a person who builds a house on a solid rock.

Matthew 7:24 NLT

Man, this is a power Scripture when you think about it. Basically, if we do things our way instead of God's way then we're not to wise and we won't see things manifest in our lives like we would like. Let's continue to listen and follow God's Word. In Jesus name, Amen!! Amen!!

Day 281: Abraham Faith

Just imagine if we developed faith like Abraham. Bible tells us no matter how old Abraham and Sarah was, they still Believe in God's promise to them.

In our impatience we often take matters into our own hands, which we hope God will bless. However, these plans often open the door for confusion and chaos. See, sometimes waiting is the best thing because it helps develop the character of God in us.

The Bible gives us promises, hope, and encouragement. God promises good to those of us who serve Him. Despite the adversity of our circumstances, God still promises good. However, we must Believe God's Word and keep our Faith working like Abraham. In Jesus name, Amen and Amen!!!!

But they that wait upon the Lord shall renew their strength; they shall mount up with wings as eagles; they shall run, and not be weary; and they shall walk, and not faint.

Isaiah 40:31 KJV

Day 282: Finding Fun And Joy

Ok, Now I know that not everything in life is necessarily enjoyable, but I think we all need to learn to have more fun in our lives. In Jesus name. And I bet if you took time to think about it every day, you could find a moment that brought you joy or laughter.

God wants us to have some fun. The Bible says a merry heart does good like medicine. I think we all need a healthy dose of laughter every day—many times during the day.

My brothers and sisters, I encourage you to look for something to smile or laugh about every day, and be sure to share a smile or a laugh with someone else and brighten their day too! In Jesus name, Amen and Amen!!!!

He will once again fill your mouth with laughter and your lips with shouts of joy.

Job 8:21 NLT

Day 283: Let The Holy Spirit Guide You; It Produces!

Scriptures says:

But the Holy Spirit produces this kind of fruit in our lives: love, joy, peace, patience, kindness, goodness, faithfulness, gentleness, and self-control. There is no law against these things!

Galatians 5:22-23 NLT

Day 284: Don't Let Your Past Hinder Or Disqualify You

Scriptures says:

No, dear brothers and sisters, I have not achieved it, but I focus on this one thing: Forgetting the past and looking forward to what lies ahead.

Philippians 3:13 NLT

Day 285: You Must Continue To Follow Him

Scriptures says:

And now, just as you accepted Christ Jesus as your Lord, you must continue to follow Him.

Colossians 2:6 NLT

Day 286: You Can't See? Stay In Faith!

Scriptures says:

For we walk by faith, not by sight.

2 Corinthians 5:7 NASB

Day 287: How Can I Worship A God I Can't Trust?

So many of us make the mistake of forgetting about God when we go through trials and tribulations, or when we feel life just isn't fair. Must we develop an attitude to trust that God is good even when life is not?

Believe it or not. But how we respond to our situations is critical and determines so much about our future. I get it: You might be saying, "man, I've been going through it for a while and it just don't look like God is anywhere to be found in my situation. It's hard to praise God or even believe." See, most of us want visible evidence and then we will praise and believe God. It doesn't work this way…

We must conclude that God is with us no matter what. The Bible tells us, not only is He *with* you, He's *for* you. And if He's for you, who can be against you?

Trust God with whatever you've been holding back. Trust Him with your future spouse. Trust Him with your children. Trust Him with your career. Trust Him with your health. Trust Him with your finances. Trust Him, Praise Him, and watch He show up and show out in every area of your life.

Let us pray:

Heavenly Father, I trust You with what I'll start and stop. I trust You with where I'll stay and go. I trust You even when I don't understand. I trust You enough to give my life to serve and connect to people. And I trust You are present with purpose in the midst of my life's storms. Thank You for being with me, guiding my steps, and giving me divine direction. Amen. Amen. In Jesus name, Amen. Thank you, Jesus!!

Day 288: Peace And More Peace

My brothers and sisters, living in God's peace is vital to enjoying life. I believe that one of the keys to living with peace in your life is taking small steps toward peace every day.

For example, spend your time wisely, don't be trying to do so many things; learn to say "no." So many of us feel like we just can't say "no." It's okay to say "no." Be careful with procrastinating. A lot of times when we procrastinate, we then put ourselves in rush mode, which can be frustrating and stressful. Pray and listen to God's Word. If you can see that your plan is not producing peace, go back to God, pray for peace and wisdom to make changes that will benefit your life.

The bottom line is to make peace a priority, take practical steps toward it, and let God lead you every day into His perfect peace that passes all understanding. In Jesus name, Amen!! Amen!!

Scriptures says:

Then you will experience God's peace, which exceeds anything we can understand. His peace will guard your hearts and minds as you live in Christ Jesus.

Philippians 4:7 NLT

Day 289: Let God Direct Our Journey

The Holy Spirit is our guide, He leads us daily. And He is always guiding us to what is best for our life. The key to a successful and enjoyable journey is to follow Him.

Ok: You may ask, "what does it mean to follow God?" Basically, it means to get in His Word, Apply His Word, and Believe His Word no matter what...

So, So, So many times we get ahead of God. We may think we know the best direction to take, or we get impatient with His timing and make a wrong turn because it looks quicker. Say what you want, but this is nothing but a setback.

However, the good news is: God is there, waiting to take the lead again and show us the right way to go. Hallelujah!!

The Lord has each of our journeys perfectly planned. We need to fully trust Him, though. As long as we can trust Him to lead us in the direction that is right for us, then Victory shall be ours in Christ Jesus. Amen!! Amen!!

Day 290: You Have To Be OK With Yourself Before It Will Be OK In Your Life

Let me explain... See, if you're not ok with yourself, you will spend so much time trying to meet the expectations of others or "keeping up with the Joneses." Don't worry about the Joneses!!!!

You might be saying, "I just can't seem to get a break. Every time I feel like I'm moving forward, I end up going backwards." Stay in God's Word and stay focused. You might be saying, "I'm overweight and it seems like no one will give me the time of day." Just trust God! Be yourself and it will happen. You might be saying, "my finances are all messed up, and I can't pay this or buy this." There's a season for everything. As long as God is First Priority in your life, then you will be simply fine.

See, a lot of times we get caught up valuing other people's lives and what they have and what they're doing. In the process of doing this we are devaluing our own life. What you think looks like Peace, Joy and Happiness. A lot of times, it's not!! Putting God first and focusing on yourself is the main thing.

Scriptures says:

Let your character or moral disposition be free from love of money [including greed, avarice, lust, and craving for earthly possessions] and be satisfied with your present [circumstances and with what you have]; for He [God] Himself has said, I will not in any way fail you nor give you up nor leave you without support. [I will] not, [I will] not, [I will] not in any degree leave you helpless nor forsake nor let [you] down (relax My hold on you)! [Assuredly not!]

Hebrews 13:5 AMPC

This means that everything will be A-ok. But God has to be at the center of it all. In Jesus name, Amen!! Amen!!!

Day 291: Being Content While God Is Working For You

See, a godly person who is content is in the best place he/she can possibly be.

Let me explain:

Joy doesn't come from having your circumstances in order and under control; it comes from what's in your heart. For example, the world is full of people who have what they THINK they want, and they're still not happy. In fact, some of the most unhappy people in the world are people who seem to "have it all."

Contentment is not about fame or being well-known, how much money you have, your position at work or your social circle. It's not found in your level of education or what side of the tracks you were born on. Contentment is a heart attitude. I mean strictly in the heart.

The word *content* means "being satisfied to the point where nothing disturbs you no matter what's going on, but not satisfied to the point that you never want any change." We all want to see things get better. But where you are right this minute doesn't have to disturb you. You can choose to believe that God is working, and things are changing, and you will see the result of it in due time. In Jesus name, Amen and Amen!!!!

Day 292: Want To Receive Your Breakthrough?

First, you need to Pray!!!

Secondly, you need to Believe God for what you are praying for. You only need to ask one time. God hears you the first time. Thirdly, while you are waiting, you need to meditate in God's Word day and night. Speak positive about your situation. This means thanking Him on a day-to-day basis about your situation. Even if it's look like nothing is working. Trust me, it's working. Continue to be patient, stay in peace and watch God work it all out for you. Your BREAKTHROUGH is right around the corner. In Jesus name, Amen!!!

I tell you, you can pray for anything, and if you believe that you've received it, it will be yours.

Mark 11:24 NLT

Study this Book of Instruction continually. Meditate on it day and night so you will be sure to obey everything written in it. Only then will you prosper and succeed in all you do.

Joshua 1:8 NLT

Day 293: Feed Your Faith, Doubt Your Doubts

Let me explain:

My brothers and sisters, we are emotional creatures. Almost all the time our actions are guided by our emotions and feelings based upon our circumstances. This causes Anger, Stress, and Doubts about our situations and circumstances. However, the Word of God is like an antidote to feed our faith, mature spiritually, and doubts our doubts.

The doctor says you won't be healed! I Doubt it; by His stripes I am healed. Someone says you're broke, and you can't get right! I Doubt it; God will supply all my needs according to His riches and glory. Folks been saying you been alone for some time now, you ain't gonna find anyone? I Doubt it; The Bible says delight myself in the Lord and He will give me the desires of my heart. Feed Your Faith, Doubt Your Doubts. In Jesus name, Amen and Amen!!!!!!

Day 294: I Speak God's Goodness To You

Scriptures says:

May the Lord bless you and protect you. May the Lord smile on you and be gracious to you. May the Lord show you His favor and give you His peace.

Numbers 6:24-26 NLT

Day 295: We Must Transform

Let me explain:

Many of us want to experience all of God's Blessings by continuing doing and living how we want to live. This won't work!!!! We must transform into what God's wants us to be and how He want us to live in order to experience all that God has for our lives.

We've got to love the Word, study the Word, and listen to the Word so it can transform us. Getting in the Word is the key to living life in the right direction. In Jesus name, Amen and Amen!!!!

Don't copy the behavior and customs of this world, but let God transform you into a new person by changing the way you think. Then you will learn to know God's will for you, which is good and pleasing and perfect.

Romans 12:2 NLT

Day 296: Stay Positive, Remember What God Has Done

Let me explain:

A whole lot of us are negative thinkers when we find ourselves in challenging situations. But to move past difficulty, we must take our negative thoughts and turn them into positive thoughts. In Jesus name!

Studying God's Word produces amazing results. It will help us get rid of those negative thoughts and give us the ability to see the positive in our situation. Being positive is powerful. And a big part of being positive is simply reminding ourselves what God is doing and what He has already done before in our lives.

If you're going through a difficult time right now, let me remind you that this probably isn't the first challenge you've faced. You've survived the last one and you will be Victorious in this one as well. Better days are on their way. God promises it!

Let us pray:

God, sometimes the situation in front of me seems impossible, but You have brought me through difficult

214

times in the past, and I know You can do it again. Help me to remember that you done it before, and you will do it again. All I need to do is trust in your Word and continue to remain positively about my present situation. In Jesus name, Amen and Amen!!!!

Day 297: You're Not Stuck, You Can Change Your Life And Experience God's Goodness

Have you ever come to a point in your life where you feel stuck, lost, tired or just don't know what else to do??? Majority of the time we feel the way we feel because we're thinking the way we're thinking. See, the issue here is that we are focusing and thinking more on our situations versus God's Word.

We can fix it though:

If you don't like where you are today in life, then change your Character! If you don't like your Character, then change your Habits! If you don't like your Habits, then change your Actions! If you don't like your Actions, then change your Decisions! If you don't like your Decisions, then change the way you Feel! If you don't like the way you Feel, then change whatever you are Exposing yourself to.

We can change and overcome whatever we may be experiencing in our lives as long as we apply God's Word and remain thinking positive. In Jesus name, Amen and Amen!!!!!!!!

Day 298: The Truth

Many of us today don't even bother to think rationally about what we believe and end up building our entire lives on beliefs that are simply not true. Whatever the news media, a celebrity or a group of friends say suddenly becomes 'truth' to us.

Believing what others say rather than exploring God's Word for ourselves will actually limit us and even keep us from doing what God created you and I to do. But only if we will contend for the truth, embrace it and build our life upon it, we will succeed in every endeavor.

If we want to stay on track with God's Truth, we have to communicate with Him frequently through prayer, reading His Word, worship, and simply acknowledging His presence and guidance throughout the day. When we get to know God, His Truth will bring peace, freedom, and joy to our lives. In Jesus name, Amen!!!!!

Let us pray:

God, I don't want to be limited by my thoughts and beliefs about what is true. You are the only source of Truth. As I spend time communicating with You, show me and guide me into Your Truth. Amen!!! Amen!!!

Day 299: The Storms Shall Pass

Some storms are quick, and some might seem like a category four hurricane! The good news is that they don't last forever, and we don't need to make major decisions in the midst of them.

I get it, we have all kinds of thoughts and feelings about our situations, but those are exactly the times we need to be careful about making decisions. We must remain calm and discipline ourselves to focus on doing what we can do and trust God to do what we can't do.

Most of us begin to stress, worry and even get angry during our stormy season. Instead of getting angry, drowning in worry and fear, we must get in touch with God, who sees past the storm.

He will make sure everything that needs to happen in our lives happens at the right time, moves at the appropriate speed, and causes us to arrive safely at the destinations He has planned for us. Amen!! Amen!!! We got to Trust Him!!! Amen and Amen!!!

Let us pray:

God, I know that I can't control everything, so I will do what I can and trust You to do what I can't do. The storms of life do not control me. I trust Your plans for me. In Jesus name, Amen!!!

Day 300: Do You Want God's Type Of Peace?

I may not know what you may be experiencing or going through right now in your life. However, the Bible tells us in John 14:27: "Peace I leave with you, my peace I give to you, not as the world giveth." Then in the same verse it says: "Let not your heart be troubled, neither be afraid."

Think about this Scripture for a second. The Bible tells us, Peace I leave with you; So, if we want peace then we can have peace. But it's up to us. Then it's tell us to not let our heart be troubled; this means we have authority to not be troubled or afraid. But again, it's up to us.

So, you see, we must go to God's Word for peace. It's the only way to overcome obstacles we face in life. We must get in the Word and stay in the Word. This allows us to become spiritual-minded, which will result in peace as well. The Word of God is spirit.

Scriptures says:

The spirit alone gives eternal life, human efforts accomplish nothing. And the very Words I have spoken to you are spirit and life.

John 6:63

My brothers and sisters, this allows us to have God's Type Of Peace!!!! Amen! Amen!!

Day 301: Nothing Is Impossible As Long As God Is At The Center

If we think positively, we can see potential in even the most discouraging situations, while those who think negatively are quick to point out problems and limitations.

Have you ever noticed how negative thinking blows things out of proportion? Problems start to seem larger and much more difficult than they really are. Sometimes, a problem may actually be impossible… in the natural. But all things are possible as long as God is at the center.

See, the whole idea of getting in the Bible and meditating on God's Word is to get rid of negative thinking and help us to refocus on who God is. And God is A Wonderful Counselor, A Way Maker, And A Miracle Worker!!!!

My brothers and sisters, we must train our brain to believe God and His Word, and experience the power available through Him. In Jesus name! We need to always remember that nothing is impossible with God at the Center. In Jesus name!

He provides Healing at the Center; He breaks Addiction at the Center; He restores Marriages at the Center; All His promises are available with Him at the Center! Amen!!! Amen !!!!

Day 302: God's Way Is The Best Way

My Brothers and Sisters we are created by God to be happy and to feel good about ourselves. If you don't feel this way, then I would encourage you to see if God is at the center of your life. As a matter of fact, we must feel good about ourselves, or eventually we will develop some sort of unhealthy, uncontrolled behavior to get the good feelings we crave. This means trouble!!!!

Think about it. A person who is addicted to drugs, Alcohol or any other kind of addiction, probably began using them because his/her pain was so intense they wanted to get rid of it. Not realizing temporary relief ends up causing a lifetime of pain and misery.

See, if we do not get good feelings from the inside, then we attempt to create them through outside means. When we go to something other than God to make us feel good about ourselves, we're really just replacing something real with a cheap substitute.

Whatever your emotional needs are today, know that only God can meet them. He is the only lasting source of life. Go to Him today, He's the only One who can satisfy.

Let us pray:

God, I don't want to waste my time chasing cheap substitutes. You are the only One who can satisfy. Show me how to daily find my true delight and satisfaction in You and only You. In Jesus name, Amen and Amen!!!!!!

Day 303: Get It Back: Your Peace, Joy, Hope, And Strength

PEACE:

> You will keep in perfect peace those whose minds are steadfast, because they trust in you.
>
> *Isaiah 26:3 NIV*

JOY:

> Until now you have not asked for anything in my name. Ask and you will receive, and your joy will be complete."
>
> *John 16:24 NIV*

HOPE:

> May the God of hope fill you with all joy and peace as you trust in Him, so that you may overflow with hope by the power of the Holy Spirit.
>
> *Romans 15:13 NIV*

STRENGTH:

> See, God has come to save me. I will trust in Him and not be afraid. The Lord GOD is my strength and my song; He has given me victory.
>
> *Isaiah 12:2 NLT*

My brothers and sisters, through Scriptures and Faith, God gives us a spirit of Peace, Joy, Hope and Strength. We can hold onto God's promises as He sees us through any situations we may find ourselves in. If for any reason you have had some doubts, I encourage you to GET IT BACK; YOUR PEACE, JOY, HOPE and STRENGTH. God will provide and He still provides. In Jesus name Amen and Amen!!!!

Day 304: Relationship, Not Religion

When you tell someone about your faith, do you give them religion... or relationship?

The Bible says we must be born again. It doesn't say we must be religious. Unfortunately, we as Christians often present the Gospel to people like it's a list of religious rules, not a true relationship with God. We got to do better...

But following "Christian" rules and going to church won't make you a Christian any more than sitting in a garage will make you a car. You must develop a personal relationship with Jesus.

If someone asks us, "What religion are you?" we should talk about our personal relationship with Jesus instead of what church we attend.

Let us pray:

God, it's easy to fall into the trap of thinking that someone needs to follow a list of rules to really be a Christian, but that's not the kind of faith You want from people. Empower me to share Your Gospel with others in a way that leads them not into a religious system, but into a one-on-one, life-changing relationship with You. In Jesus name, Amen!! Amen!!

Day 305: God Really Wants To Bless Us

If you have asked God for something and He hasn't given it to you yet, rest assured that He is not holding out on you. He simply wants to make sure that you make Him your top priority.

God wants us to prosper in every way. He wants people to see His goodness and how well He takes care of us. But we must desire God more than we desire His blessings.

If for some reason you feel like God has forgotten you; don't worry, He hasn't. Continue to stay in God's Word, Believe God's Word, and Act upon God's Word. And watch God Bless you in whatever it is you are believing God for. In Jesus name Amen!!!

Scriptures says:

Seek the Kingdom of God above all else, and live righteously, and He will give you everything you need.

Matthew 6:33 NLT

Day 306: The Blessing Of The Lord

Difficulties and temptation are facts of life for everyone. As we face difficult times though, our attitude can make all the difference...

Peace, Healing, Favor, Victory, Joy, Prosperous, Provision for every area of your life... Speak the words into existence!!!!!!!

Scriptures says:

God blessed those who patiently endure testing and temptation. Afterwards they will receive the crown of life that God has promised to those who love Him.

James 1:12 NLT

Day 307: You Will Rise

Scriptures says:

But if you pray to God and seek the favor of the Almighty, and if you are pure and live with integrity, He will surely rise up and restore your happy home. And though you started with little, you will end with much.

Job 8:5-7 NLT

Let us pray:

Father, I ask You to give me complete understanding of what You want to do in my life, I ask You to make me wise with spiritual wisdom. Then the way I live will always honor and please You, and I will continually do good, kind things for others. All the while, I will learn to know You better and better. I roll my works upon You, Lord and You make my thoughts agreeable to Your will, so my plans are established and succeed. And by this we shall continue to Rise Up. In Jesus name, Amen!! Amen!!

Day 308: Relying On God For Real

Look!!! Don't say you're Trusting, and Believing God cause it sound good and religious. This won't help you see results in your life.

Think about it, every time we feel frustration, it means we've really stopped RELYING on God. We have stopped trusting and believing. See, frustration hits when we stop depending on Him and try to make something happen ourselves.

I do realize that depending on God for everything may be difficult, but it's the key to the victory we need every single day of our lives.

Be REAL with yourself today, "What am I doing with my faith?" Are you putting your faith in yourself, or in others, or in your circumstances? That's not living in grace, that's just living by your own strength and works. And it won't get the job done!!!!!!! We must Rely on God For Real....

Once you release your faith and trust God to do what you can't do, you're putting your faith in Him and this is aligning yourself with God's Word.

God, I know that life won't always go the way I want it to, but I trust in You. By faith, I receive Your grace, the power You have freely given to help me walk through any situation I face today. Amen Amen!!!!!!!!!

Day 309: Get Rid Of The Wilderness Mentality

The Israelites wandered around in the wilderness for forty years. But the journey was only supposed to be an eleven-day journey. Why?

The Israelites couldn't move on because they had a "wilderness mentality." They wanted to do things their way instead of God's way. My brothers and sisters, most of us are doing the same thing today. We're looking for Godly results our way and it doesn't work like that.

Which means we keep on going around the same mountains instead of making progress, and it takes us years to experience victory over something that could have been dealt with quickly. My! My! My! My!

We need a new mindset y'all. We need to start believing that God's Word is true. Matthew 19:26 tells us that with God all things are possible. All He needs is our faith in Him. He needs for us to believe, and He will do the rest. Let's get rid of that Wilderness Mentality. It's time for us to move on! In Jesus name, Amen!!!!!!

Let us pray:

Lord, continue to help me renew my mind and create in me a clean heart. I've spent enough time going around the

226

same old mountains in my life. With You, I know I can move on, so I put my faith in You and let go of my wilderness mentality!! In Jesus name, Amen and Amen!!!! Hallelujah!!

Day 310: We Shall Live By Faith

My brothers and sisters, living by faith is probably one of the hardest things to do during our journey with Christ. In Hebrews 10:38, Bible says: Now the just shall live by faith: but if any man draw back, my soul shall have no pleasure in him. We are considered the "just" if you've been born again.

See, Faith is simply our positive response to God's Grace. Faith is not something you do to get God to respond. God has already responded. He has provided everything we will ever need. Faith comes by believing that my situation will work out even when it looks like a mess.

Right believing equals right living and right living equals manifestation. It's not a matter of how big or little your faith is. The question is, will you keep it working??

Most of us believe that our performances will gain favor with God. Not true!! Grace is undeserved favor. A lot of folks try to figure out when will God do this and that. He's already done it. We spend more time doing instead of believing. Then we become drained, frustrated, irritated, stressed, worried and everything else... Stay close to God, Stay in His Word, Believe His Word, Remain In Faith and watch God show up and show out. In Jesus name, Amen and Amen!!!

And it is impossible to please God without faith. Anyone who wants to come to Him must believe that God exists and that He rewards those who sincerely seek Him.

Hebrews 11:6 NLT

Day 311: Don't Give in to Self-Pity

Self-pity is a destructive and negative emotion. It blinds us to our blessings and the possibilities before us as well as stealing our hope for both today and tomorrow.

Self-pity is actually idolatry because it is self-focus carried to the extreme. When we allow ourselves to fall into self-pity, we are essentially rejecting God's love and His ability to change things.

I encourage you not to waste one more day of your life in self-pity. God has thoughts and plans for your good, to give you hope for your future.

Let us pray:

God, I refuse to feel sorry for myself. Even if things are difficult right now, I know that You are bigger than my problems and that You have a good future planned for me. In Jesus name, Amen!!!!!!

Day 312: If You Trust, You Will Not Lack

Scriptures says:

Even strong young lions sometimes go hungry, but those who trust in the Lord will lack no good thing.

Psalms 34:10 NLT

Day 313: Take It One Day At A Time; You Can Do It!

Don't live your life without the thrill of growing and changing, or you'll miss out on the good things God can do through you.

Take some time today to visualize the person you want to be and start pursuing God's freedom. Because one day at a time, you and God can anything.

So, keep a positive attitude no matter where you are right now, no matter what's going on in your life. Cheer up, God is on your side. Stop being upset about things you can't do anything about.

Scriptures says:

For I can do everything through Christ, who strengthens me.

Philippians 4:13 NLT

Day 314: Pursue It!

Let me explain:

God wants to bless us in every which way possible. He want us to Rest in His Word! He wants us to be Healed! He want us to Prosper! He want us to have Peace! He want us to get the Victory! Pursue it and receive it!!!!

Scriptures says:

But you, Timothy, are a man of God; so, run from all these evil things. Pursue righteousness and a godly life, along with faith, love, perseverance, and gentleness.

1 Timothy 6:11 NLT

Let us pray:

Lord, in everything I do, I want to serve You wholeheartedly. Thank You for encouraging me to Pursue, to step out and take action, developing the great potential You have given me to be successful in every area of my life. I speak Peace, Wisdom, Spiritual Maturity, Deliverance, Victory, Joy, Favor, and Healing right now in Jesus name. All IS WELL!! In Jesus name, Amen and Amen!!!!!

Day 315: Make God Your Source Of Approval

Let's think for a moment. If we're not making God our source, then there are some insecurity issues somewhere.

One result of insecurity is our Faith, Hope, and Joy of life being stole and causing major problems in relationships with others and with God. We who are insecure, often seek the approval of others to try to overcome our feelings of rejection, low self-worth, pain, depression, and etc. We should not allow this...

When we struggle with insecurity, only one thing will set us free, and that is God's truth. The truth is that we don't need to struggle to get from man what God freely gives us: love, acceptance, approval, security, worth, and value. Bible says He is our refuge and strength and always ready to help in times of trouble.

As we look to Him, we will be lifted to new levels of freedom, becoming the confident, mature person we were created to be in Christ Jesus... Amen!! Amen!!

Let us pray:

Lord, I look to You for security. I focus on the truth - You are my refuge and strength. You give me love and acceptance. In You alone I am completely confident. In Jesus name, Amen!!!!

Day 316: Meditate And Ponder God's Word

Ok: If we really want to be the men and women God wants us to be, we must take time to really think about God's Word. There's power in the Word! There is deliverance in the Word! There's healing in the Word! Getting and staying in God's Word is not always an easy task for everyone, but without God's Word, our lives will never reach the full potential of what God desires for us.

To meditate and Ponder on God's Word, we must do this:

- We must Obey God's Word!
- Hide God's Word in our heart!
- Speak confession of Faith!
- Rejoice in His Word!
- Study God's Word!
- Reflect on His ways, not ours!

BELIEVE HIS WORD!! In Jesus name Amen and Amen!!!!

Scriptures says:

Teach me your decrees, O Lord; I will keep them to the end. Give me understanding and I will obey your instructions; I will put them into practice with all my heart. Make me walk along the path of your commands, for that is where my happiness is found.

Psalms 119:33-35 NLT

Day 317: Why Settle?

Let me explain:

I think a lot of times we really don't know our value or self-worth. But I believe if we stay with the Word of God we will realize and know our worth and value.

Throughout our lives, we tend to do a lot of settling, whether it's a job, relationship, or even when it's come to the Word of God. A lot of Christians or Believers tend to settle in their Christian journey and don't experience all that God has for them.

For I can do everything through Christ, who gives me strength.

Philippians 4:13 NLT

And this same God who takes care of me will supply all your needs from His glorious riches, which have been given to us in Christ Jesus.

Philippians 4:19 NLT

The thief cometh not, but for to steal, and to kill, and to destroy I am come that they might have life, and that they might have it more abundantly.

John 10:10 KJV

These are just a few examples of God's Word. Let's start saying and believing what His Word says. This way we don't have to settle, and we can experience all that God has for us. In Jesus name, Amen and Amen!!!!

Day 318: Understand Grace, Walk By Faith

Now, this is so powerful my brothers and sisters. Most of us are aware that it is by grace that we are saved, but I wonder how many people really understand the power of God's grace.

Everything we receive from God must come by grace through faith. Which means Grace makes and Faith takes. See, God has provided everything here on earth we will ever need to enjoy a fruitful life. All we have to do is get into agreement with God's Word by Believing His Word, and receive all that Grace has made available.

I know back in the day we were taught that you had to do good in order for God to be good to you. That's incorrect. Let's remember, we're not doing good just to receive favors from God. Deep down in our heart we should be trusting God's Word, Believing God's Word, and Applying God's Word because of our LOVE for God.

God's Grace is undeserved favor. It's free. Just Believe it and receive it. When you understand grace, you can walk in faith and receive God's blessings. Everything in the Bible, salvation, the infilling of the Holy Spirit, fellowship with God and all victory in our daily lives, is based on it. Let's continue to walk by faith and not by sight, and experience the goodness of the Lord because He first loved us. In Jesus name.

Let us pray:

God, Help me to understand how wonderful Your grace is so that my faith in You can grow. In Jesus name, Amen and Amen!!!!!

Day 319: Getting What You Don't Deserve

Let me explain:

Most folks allow God to help them only when they think they deserve it. This is wrong thinking!! This kind of thinking doesn't produce an attitude of gratitude and thanksgiving. If we think we deserve what we receive, then it is no longer a gift but a reward or "payment for services rendered."

See, Grace is undeserved favor. A free gift from God. We don't do anything to deserve it.

My brothers and sisters, I encourage you to open your heart and allow God's grace to come into your life to help you in your everyday walk. Always remember that when you feel frustrated, it is because you are living by your own effort and need to get back into God's grace by allowing Him to work through you. In Jesus name, Amen and Amen!!!!

Let us pray:

Lord, I realize the foolishness of only accepting Your help when I feel like I deserve it; this is the wrong way to think. I give up on my own works, and receive Your grace. Thank You for helping me in every situation, even when I don't deserve it. Amen!! Amen!!

Day 320: Do It Your Way? No! Do It God's Way? Yes!

Scriptures says:

Therefore, they must eat the bitter fruit of living their own way, choking on their own schemes.

Proverbs 1:31 NLT

But all who listen to me will live in peace, untroubled by fear of harm.

Proverbs 1:33 NLT

Let's meditate on these two Scriptures. The first Scripture basically tells us that doing things our way will cause heartache, pain, stress, dis-ease, diseases, and the possibility of death. All of these are opposite of what God has planned for our lives. I will say it's a choice, though.

The second Scripture basically tells us that doing things God's way will allow us to experience peace, joy, happiness strength and etc.…

My brothers and sisters Let's do it God's way and experience His best. In Jesus name, Amen!!

Day 321: Let God Do The Heavy Lifting

Too many times we see what's wrong with ourselves and try to fix it through our own strength, but this will never be good enough. Jesus said in John 15:5 NIV: "Apart from me you can do nothing."

We may try to be self-sufficient, but we need to let God supply the grace and ability to do what we need to do. Willpower and determination can get us started, but they've been known to quit in the middle and leave us stranded.

We can learn to enjoy the life Jesus died to give us by inviting God to become involved in every aspect of it.

We are not made to function without God. And with Him, we can break any bad habit or addiction, like overeating, substance abuse, poor time management, anger issues, you name it. Jesus is bigger than any problem you have.

Let us pray:

God, I know that I'm nothing without You, so I invite You into every area of my life. I'll let You do the heavy lifting, following and trusting You every day. Amen Amen!!!!

Day 322: Where You Are Weak, God Is Strong

If we could let God be God, then we would be so much better off. The only way to overcome our weakness is to rely on God's strength. To do that, we have to stop focusing on our weakness and focus on our strength in Christ Jesus.

Jesus did not come to earth, die on the cross, and rise again on the third day for us to be weak and defeated. He came so that we might have life more abundantly.

So, the next time you find yourself confronted by your weakness, remember and declare that where you are weak, He is strong! Amen! Amen!

Let us pray:

God, I declare and confess that where I am weak, You are strong. So, I will not worry about, or remain defeated by, my weakness. Instead, I put my faith in Your strength.

Day 323: Cry Out To God!

Let me explain:

Our Lord God should be included in everything. He should be first priority in our lives. We need to continue to Pray, Study God's Word and Believe God's Word.

Life can be so hard, so difficult; at times, it can be overwhelming. Especially when dealing with Unemployment, Financial Challenges, Depression, Stress, Health issues, Addiction, Discouragement, Loneliness, and etc....

All we have to do is call upon the Lord, Cry out to the Lord and Seek the Lord. The Bible tells us that, "The Lord is my rock and my fortress and my deliverer, my God, my rock, in whom I take refuge, my shield, and the horn of my salvation, my stronghold."

- When troubled, cry out: the Lord is my rock.
- When discouraged, cry out: the Lord is my stronghold.
- When weary, cry out: the Lord is my strength.
- When fearful, cry out: the Lord is my deliverer.
- When overwhelmed, cry out: the Lord is my fortress.
- When worried, cry out: the Lord is my refuge.
- When alone, cry out: the Lord will make a way.

For every need, on every occasion, cry out to God, who is our rock and our refuge. In Jesus name, Amen and Amen!!

Day 324: The Bible Is Alive

Let me explain:

At times, we're frustrated, stressed and we grow weary. We are confused, discouraged, and lonely. We struggle with doubts and fears. We battle disappointment and anger, guilt and shame. My brothers and sisters, whenever you find yourself In any and all of these dark times, run to God and

His Word. Let the Word of God wash over you, cleanse you, heal you, deliver you, prosper you. Whatever you do, allow God's Word to continue to penetrate deep down in your heart because His Word is Definitely Alive. In Jesus name, Amen and Amen!!!

Scriptures says:

The instructions of the Lord are perfect, reviving the soul. The decrees of the Lord are trustworthy, making wise the simple.

Psalms 19:7 NLT

Study this Book of Instruction continually. Meditate on it day and night so you will be sure to obey everything written in it. Only then will you prosper and succeed in all you do.

Joshua 1:8 NLT

Day 325: Trusting In God Is The Only Way

My brothers and sisters, we all encounter a number of challenges and burdens, and sometimes these problems feel overwhelming. Whether it's Unemployment, financial pressure, depression, a rebellious teenager, the death of a loved one, a difficult decision, a feeling of failure, health related issues, trouble in a marriage, and etc.

Bible tells us in the book of John: Jesus taught us that we would face tribulations in this world. The real issue is, how will we respond?

When we face these challenges, do we Trust In God, or do we trust in other things? Do we trust our own efforts, our own resources, and our own thinking? Do we first look to other people to guide us, rescue us, or protect us? Do we rely on our careful research, our diligent efforts, our network, and our abilities? Or are we Trusting God.

Don't mistake me, God can use any of these things, of course, and He frequently does. But in our heart of hearts, where is our trust? Where is our confidence? If it's not in God FIRST, then we will be fighting an uphill battle.

My brothers and sisters, I encourage you to First Trust God and He will guide you through. TRUSTING GOD IS THE ONLY WAY!! In Jesus name, Amen and Amen!!!!

Scriptures says:

Trust in the Lord with all your heart; do not depend on your own understanding. Seek His will in all you do, and He will show you which path to take.

Proverbs 3:5-6 NLT

Day 326: God Will Raise You Out And Up

In John 11:21-24, Jesus visited Mary and Martha after their brother Lazarus had been dead for four days. When He finally arrived, Martha said, "Master, if You had been here, my brother would not have died." Then Jesus said to her: "Your brother shall rise again." Martha replied: "I know that he will rise again in the resurrection at the last day."

Now when you break this down, I don't think Martha really understood what Jesus was saying. She was looking toward a future possibility, not a present reality. She didn't really expect things to change.

See, a lot of us are like Martha, stuck in our situations, circumstances and troubles, not realizing that God can turn things around in the NOW if we Believe.

Just continue to stay in faith. Don't lose hope. You might be hurting now, but out of every disaster, God can bring a new beginning. All we have to do is Meditate on God's Word, Believe in God, Apply His Word and watch Him show His glory in our lives. All things are possible with God. In Jesus name, Amen!!!

Scriptures says:

Jesus responded, "Didn't I tell you that you would see God's glory if you believe?"

John 11:40 NLT

Day 327: Practice Being Thankful

We all know that we should be grateful for our many blessings. Because deep down inside God has been good to each of us even in a time of need. God tells us in His Word to be thankful, and we know from our own experience that once we seriously start praising God, our burdens and troubles seem to weigh less heavily on our shoulders.

David said, "I will bless the Lord at all times; His praise shall continually be in my mouth." This is basically letting God know: Lord I Thank You and I give you the Glory and the Praise.

We need to be more like David. When we do this, not only does it help set us free, but as we pause to give thanks to God for the blessings we enjoy in our lives, we actually begin to find more blessings, even more to be thankful for!

I encourage you, my brothers and sisters, to take time to practice being thankful. There is so much for us to be grateful for, and we need to focus on it every single day.

Let us pray:

Dear God, Thank You for blessing me daily and working in my life. I know that without You, I have nothing, so I thank You for the goodness that You have shown me. In Jesus name, Amen and Amen!!!!!

Day 328: The Lord Is Our Strength

See, we must realize that part of Satan's plan for believers is to make us weary. Hold on!! Wait a minute!

Scriptures says:

For I can do everything through Christ, who gives me strength.

Philippians 4:13 NLT

Yet amid all these things we are more than conquerors and gain a surpassing victory through Him Who loved us.

Romans 8:37 AMP

Both of these Scriptures tells us that we all good, we already won, if we believe it. Amen somebody!!

See, we must propose in our hearts to maintain such an intimate relationship with God through prayer and His Word that we are constantly being strengthened by the power of His promises. Being connected with God produces strong Christians or believers who can outlast the devil!

242

Live your life totally confident in God's strength and have no fear of the trials, worries and situations that can produce weariness. Remain strong "in Him" and in the power of His might, and we shall overcome. Amen!! Amen!!

Let us pray:

God, You alone are my strength. I won't let Satan make me a weary Christian, but I'll remain strong in you at all times. In Jesus name, Amen and Amen!!!

Day 329: We Are Equipped For Success

Let us pray:

Father, I thank you for the spirit of Power, Love, Calmness, a Well-balanced mind, Discipline, and Self Control. In the name of Jesus, I walk out of the realm of failure into the arena of success, giving thanks to you Lord. Thank you for the Grace to remain diligent in seeking knowledge and skills in areas where I am inexperienced. Father, I will withstand the devil. I will hold firm in my faith, rooted, established, strong immovable and determined. I shall mediate on your Word day and night, for then I will make my way prosperous and have good SUCCESS. Thank you, Lord. In the name of Jesus, Amen!!!!

Day 330: There's Only One Problem-Solver: Jesus

See, if we are NOT willing to Trust, Believe and Obey God in Jesus Christ, we soon become enslaved to something else such as drugs, alcohol, sexual activity, work, or even bad religious practices.

These things can never solve our problems. Let's be honest, depending upon anything else other than God leads to even deeper problems. Only God can offer us the power to be delivered from bondage to build new lives, experience joy, peace and happiness. Turning to God and believing in Christ Jesus is the way. In Jesus name, Amen and Amen!!!

Scriptures says:

Commit everything you do to the Lord. Trust Him, and He will help you.

Psalms 37:5 NLT

Day 331: Value Yourself, Know Your Self-Worth

You may not think highly of yourself, but God wants you to like who you are.

1. Never speak negatively about yourself. Say what the Word of God says about you by

acknowledging every good thing in you through Christ Jesus, not by focusing on the wrong.

2. Don't do it! Stop! I mean Stop comparing yourself to others. Run your race. Things will work out for you just as they are already planned. Keep God First though.

3. Let God determine your worth. Remember that you have already been accepted by God.

4. Remember, NONE of us are perfect. Keep your flaws in perspective. It's ok to see where you want to improve, but make sure you appreciate your progress. If not, you will continue to beat yourself up and this will get you nowhere.

5. Discover the true source of confidence. If you place your confidence in God, you can't help but have Joy, Peace and Happiness. Trust, Believe and leave the results to Him. In Jesus name, Amen and Amen!!!

Let us pray:

God, thank You for accepting me even when I have trouble accepting myself. Help me to acknowledge the good qualities You've given me and keep my flaws in perspective as I find my confidence in You. Thank you, Jesus. Amen!!! Amen!!!

Day 332: Dealing With Setbacks, Confusion, And Disappointments

See, it's not God's will for us to live a confused, disappointed, devastated, or oppressed life today, or any day.

Think about all the people who encountered Jesus in the Bible. Whether they were stressed, worried, tired, sick, confused angered or disappointed; they found new hope when they encountered the power of Jesus. Likewise, we need to do the same. This same power is available to us today.

All we need to do is start focusing on God, meditating on His promises, confessing His Word, and submitting ourselves and our situation to Him in prayer. Through Jesus, we can fight the enemy's attempts to weigh us down, rebuking him so that he can't destroy us.

Let us pray:

Lord God, setbacks and discouraging things will come my way, but I will not remain confused, angered, worried, stressed, or disappointed. I will continue to trust in your Word because I know with your power that resides in me, I will handle anything that's need to be handled for my good. As I stay tuned-in to You, I will fight off the devil and send him running every time. In Jesus name, Amen!!!!

Day 333: Know The Word

Maybe you have been wondering why it always seems that you are under attack, facing one problem or another, and don't have victory in your life. Perhaps you need to spend more time abiding in the Word of God.

Many believers and non-believers go to church every week to listen to someone else preach the Word to them, but they never know the Word for themselves. See, if you want to live in peace, joy and victory, you must give God's Word a place of priority in your everyday life. You have to make this a lifestyle, not just once or twice a week thing.

You might ask, "How does this work?" You can confess the Word while you get ready in the morning. Maybe you could listen to teaching or worship music on the way to work, or just throughout the day on a daily basis. Pray and read the Word of God. These are just a few ideas for applying God's Word in your life so that you can experience all that God has for you and me. Amen!! Amen!!

Scriptures says:

I have written to you who are God's children because you know the Father. I have written to you who are mature in the faith because you know Christ, who existed from the beginning. I have written to you who are young in the faith because you are strong. God's Word lives in your hearts, and you have won your battle with the evil one.

1 John 2:14 NLT

Lord, I want to make sure that I apply Your Word into my life. I want to agree with your Word. I don't just want to hear someone tell me the Word once a week, I want to know it for myself. In Jesus name, Amen and Amen!!!!!!

Day 334: God Will Supply

Scriptures says:

But my God shall supply all your need according to His riches in glory by Christ Jesus.

Philippians 4:19 KJV

Day 335: God's Type Of Love

Let me explain:

Have you ever felt unloved? Do you want to experience true love? Long lasting love? Temporary love won't cut it. See, a lot of times we are looking for fulfillment in ways that seem good at first but often leave us feeling frustrated, disappointed and empty inside. This is temporary love.

Does this ever happen to you? Do you ever look for love and end up feeling unfulfilled? Let me ask you this: What kind of love are you pursuing?

You may be looking for love, but really, you're looking for God type of love, because He is love. However, you must be connected to God to experience His true love. If not, you are just resorting back to temporary love, which will

248

leave you feeling unfulfilled, lonely, hurt, depressed, sad, angered, and etc....

The Bible says that in Him we live, move, and have our being. That tells me that without Him, life is not complete. Aww man, this is powerful!!!!

Everyone is looking for love, but are you looking for God's type of love? It's the only love that matters, the only love that lasts, and the only love that fulfills.

Let us pray:

Lord, I don't want to spend my life unfulfilled, pursuing love that's not from You. If it's not found in You, it's not real love, because You are love. Today, I find my love in You. In Jesus name, Amen and Amen!!!!

Day 336: Speak God's Word To Your Situations And Circumstances

In the Bible, when Jesus said that we are to speak to the mountain, commanding it to be lifted up and thrown into the sea, He was giving us the blueprint to overcome our situations and circumstances.

See, we usually spend too much time complaining, worrying, and talking about the "mountains," or challenges, in our lives, but God's Word instructs us to talk to them. And when we do, we must respond to them with the Word of God. In Jesus name!

Whenever trials and tribulations occur in our lives, we need to confess Scriptures on our situations. Here's the issue: majority of us want to see immediate results and when we don't, we stop speaking the Word of God, and resort right back to our flesh, wondering why the situation hasn't changed or gotten better. Constantly speaking the Word is powerful and absolutely necessary in overcoming any problem or negative situation. Amen!!!

Let us pray:

Lord, I just want to thank you for all that you have done, all that you are doing and all that you're getting ready to do in my life. I thank you for giving me wisdom and strength to speak your Word daily over my situation and circumstances. Lord I realize that I need you. In order to receive manifestation, I must enter into a resting place. Lord I realize when I rest, then you will work. This way I will have peace, comfort, strength, joy, and victory over my situations and circumstances. I thank you Lord. In Jesus name, Amen and Amen!!!!!!!!!

Day 337: Keep A Positive Attitude; You Shall Overcome!

Don't live your life without the thrill of growing and changing, or you'll miss out on the good things God can do through you.

Take some time today to visualize the person you want to be, and start pursuing God's freedom. Because one day at a time, you and God can accomplish anything.

So, keep a positive attitude no matter where you are right now, no matter what's going on in your life. Cheer up, God is on your side. All you have to do is Stay in His Word and Believe His Word. Stop being upset about things you can't do anything about.

Scriptures says:

For I can do everything through Christ, who gives me strength.

Philippians 4:13 NLT

Day 338: Are You Willing To Commit To The Lord?

You Should!!!!! Trust Him with it all… Your problems, your situations, your issues, your circumstances, your troubles, your fears, your unbelief, your hurt, your past, your addiction, your health, your career, your job, your marriage, your decisions, and your life. In Jesus name, Amen and Amen!!

Scriptures says:

Commit everything you do to the Lord. Trust Him, and He will help you.

Psalms 37:5 NLT

Day 339: Look To Jesus, He's The Answer

Scriptures says:

If you look for me wholeheartedly, you will find me.

Jeremiah 29:13 NLT

Day 340: Casting All Your Care

Scriptures says:

Casting all your care upon Him; for He careth for you.

1 Peter 5:7 KJV

Okay, think about this Scripture for a second. When was the last time you really cast all your care on the Lord? See, I'm not talking about giving your problems to God for a few days or months. I'm talking about casting *all* your care to the Lord.

When a situation arises, you give it to God and say, "All is well, you got it Lord." Don't think about it anymore. If the situation pops back up in your mind again, you repeat the same thing again. "All is well, you got it Lord." You might be asking, "how many times do I have to cast my care?" As many times as you need to until you have meditated on God's Word and Believe His Word whereas the situation now becomes a non-factor to you.

When you do this, you are now demonstrating Rest. When you rest in God's Word, I promise you Manifestation will take place in whatever areas or situations in your life.

Here's the question: Is you gonna do it? You might be saying right now, "I'm gonna do it, I'm going to cast all my care." But then your spouse continue to keep doing the same things y'all have issues with, you just got a negative report from the doctor, or you thought you had a breakthrough only to realize it wasn't. Someone said they were going to bless you financially and they didn't. You thought you had a job opportunity lined up, but it didn't

252

come through. Whatever your situations may be. Are you going to cast your care? You must replace your care with God's Word. Lay your burdens down, stop thinking about it, move forward and trust God. In Jesus name, Amen and Amen!!!!

Day 341: Experience God's Prosperity

Some folks have issues with prosperity and some even say it's not biblical. But God wants us all to prosper and enjoy prosperity in every area of our lives. Remember, prosperity is not just financial. It's also joy, favor, peace, healing, strength, victory, and etc. See, when we prosper, God gets the Glory and we can let everyone know that "God did this, and if He did it for me, He can do it for you."

Scriptures says:

Let them shout for joy, and be glad, that favor my righteous cause: yea, let them say continually, Let the Lord be magnified, which hath pleasure in the prosperity of His servant.

Psalms 35:27 KJV

The blessing of the Lord makes a person rich, and He adds no sorrow with it.

Proverbs 10:22 KJV

Remember the Lord your God. He is the one who gives you power to be successful in order to fulfill the covenant He confirmed to your ancestors with.

Deuteronomy 8:18 NLT

You know the generous grace of our Lord Jesus Christ. Though he was rich, yet for your sakes He became poor, so that by His poverty He could make you rich.

2 Corinthians 8:9 NLT

So you see, God wants us all to prosper in every area of our lives. All we need to do is agree with God's Word and apply it and wait for the manifestation. I speak prosperity to each of you. In Jesus name, Amen! Amen!

Day 342: Reaching Out To Others

Reaching out to others isn't something we should pay lip service to. It should be a top priority of living the Christian life.

It takes determination and commitment to stretch ourselves to help others, but that's how God wants us to live. God says that when you truly give and pour yourself out for others, He will use you.

Scriptures says:

Your light shall dawn in the darkness and your darkness shall be as the noonday.

Isaiah 58:10 NKJV

If you reach beyond your own situation and bring Christ's love to others, the circumstances you face will fade away and disappear. And you'll experience the wondrous joy of making a difference where it counts.

What if you decide to change, to make this the time in your life when you make a difference? Rearrange your priorities today and reach out to others.

Let us pray:

Lord, I want to readjust my priorities and reach out to others the way You want me to. Help me as I step out with determination to make a difference for You. Amen and Amen!!

Day 343: Abiding In God's Word

Most Christians or Believers know the importance of reading the Bible, but many do not understand the importance of abiding in the Word and allowing the Word to abide in them.

When we meditate and study the Word and hide Scripture verses in our hearts, we have instant access to them whenever we need them. The Bible tells us that we can ask for whatever we need in prayer and receive it. In Jesus name!

Abiding in the Word and allowing the Word to abide in us makes us true disciples of Jesus. Why? Because we now are developing a relationship with Jesus rather than just being religious. Abiding in the Word also gives us more power in our prayer lives, which in return gives us power over the enemy.

My brothers and sisters, I encourage you to make reading and studying the Word a priority. Start memorizing Scriptures and hiding them in your heart. Then, when you face the battles of life, you will be fully armed and prepared to win the war with the Shield Of Faith by fighting off them fiery darts the devil throws at you. In Jesus name, Amen!!!!

Lord, I want to be a true disciple and walk in the power that comes from abiding in Your Word. Lead me as I diligently study your Word and hide Your truth down in my heart. In Jesus name, Amen!!!!

Day 344: Forgetting About Ourselves

Paul said that he had been "crucified with Christ." In other words, he had to stop thinking about himself in order to live for God. And we are encouraged to do the same.

At this point you may be thinking, "What about me? Who is going to take care of me?" This is usually what prevents us from living the way God wants us to live. We are always thinking about ourselves.

We are so accustomed to seeing our desires satisfied that the very thought of forgetting about ourselves even for one day can be frightening.

The secret to having freedom and joy is giving your life away rather than trying to keep it. When you get the focus off of you and onto God, God can show you how to live a truly meaningful life.

I encourage you to start your days by dedicating yourself to God and others. When you do, He will faithfully help you live a godly life.

Let us pray:

Lord, I offer You my eyes, ears, mouth, hands, feet, heart, finances, gifts, talents, abilities, time, energy, all of me! It's not about me. It's all about You. Amen!!!

Day 345: We Have The Power, Flip The Switch

My brothers and sisters this is so critical.

Scriptures says:

> Now unto him that is able to do exceedingly abundantly above all that we ask or think, according to the power that worketh in us.
>
> *Ephesians 3:20*

This Scripture tells us that we have the power, but we must exercise it. If you walk into a dark room, it will stay dark unless you flip the light switch on. Likewise, we must exercise the power we have by utilizing God's Word.

> He who conceals his transgressions will not prosper, But whoever confesses and turns away from his sins will find compassion and mercy.
>
> *Proverbs 28:13*

This means we have the POWER to confess God's Word over our situations and circumstances!!!

> Commit everything you do to the Lord. Trust Him, and He will help you.
>
> *Psalm 37:5*

This means we have the POWER to commit!!!!

> Don't let your hearts be troubled. Trust in God, and trust also in me.
>
> *John 14:1*

This means we have the POWER to not let our heart be troubled and we need to Trust in the Lord.!!!!!

This is my command–be strong and courageous! Do not be afraid or discouraged. For the Lord your God is with you wherever you go.

Joshua 1:9

This means we have the POWER to believe God's Word, be strong and courageous!!!!!

These are just a few Scriptures to indicate that no matter what we may be going through we have the power to overcome it all. However, we must FLIP THE SWITCH!!!! In Jesus name, Amen!!!!

Day 346: Don't Be So Busy! Make God The First Priority In Your Life

In today's society, we are so busy with our lives, jobs, families and a whole bunch of other stuff that we tend to neglect God and put God second. GOD SHOULD BE FIRST PRIORITY!!!!!!!!

When you have the Word of God in abundance, you have more of it inside you than anything else! You're so full of the Word that when trouble comes, the Word is the first thing out of your mouth.

So, fix your mind on the Word of God every day. Apply it to yourself, personally. Then place yourself in agreement with what God says about you in that Word. Make up your mind that you are who God says you are. You can do what God says you can do. And you can have what He says you can have. Put yourself in agreement with Him, then receive it.

God promises that if you'll keep His Word in front of you, if you'll put it first place in your life, you'll know how to prosper and succeed in all you do. In Jesus name, Amen!! Amen!!

Day 347: What Happens When You Trust The Lord?

Scriptures says:

But those who trust in the Lord will find new strength. They will soar high on wings like eagles. They will run and not grow weary. They will walk and not faint.

Isaiah 40:31 NLT

Day 348: What Happens When You Remain In God?

Scriptures says:

But if you remain in me and my words remain in you, you may ask for anything you want, and it will be granted!

John 15:7 NLT

Day 349: A Reminder Of What True Love Is

Scriptures says:

Love is patient and kind. Love is not jealous or boastful or proud or rude. It does not demand its own way. It is not irritable, and it keeps no record of being wronged.

1 Corinthians 13:4-5 NLT

Day 350: He Never Stops Working

Aww man! This is so powerful, my brothers and sisters. God never stops working. He's always working on our behalf.

Even when we can't see it, He's working!! Even when we can't feel it, He's working!! Even when our lives are a mess, He's working!! Even when relationships and marriages are broken, He's working!!! See, no matter what, God is always working. We need to thank Him and Praise Him in the midst of it all.

The Bible tells us in Psalms 34, "I will praise the Lord at all times. I will constantly speak His praises." So even if you can't see God moving on your behalf, or you can't feel Him moving on your behalf, just know that He's always working, and He never stops working. We must continue to Praise Him. In Jesus name, Amen!!!!

Dear Lord, I just want to say thank you. I know at times it doesn't seem like or feel like you're working on my behalf, but truth be told, you've been right by my side all along. No matter what, Lord, I will continue to thank you and praise you. You been too good to me. You've been better to me than I been to myself, and I want to say Thank you Lord!!!! Thank you for always being there every step of the way. In Jesus name, Amen!!!!

Day 351: We Can Win The Battle

Let me explain:

Right now, you and I are in the middle of a spiritual war. As long as we live in this world, we are going to have to resist becoming like it. Yes! I know it's a daily battle, and sadly, the church today is full of worldly, carnal, fleshly believers, which makes it even more difficult. But if we want to live in a way that can change our world, then we have to stop living in the flesh and start living in the Spirit.

Every one of us needs to continually adjust; put our fleshly desires under the Holy Spirit's control, and not let our emotions or mind rule us. The devil is constantly working overtime trying to make sure that we give in to the flesh, to prevent us from winning the battle.

Ultimately, we decide who wins the battle in our life. We don't have to be the subject of our flesh. We can live in the Spirit, bringing our flesh in line with His Will. We can win the battle today my brothers and sisters. Amen!! Amen!!!

God, I thank you that the battle has already been won. My flesh will lead to heartache, pain, stress, confusion discomfort, and possibility of death, but living in Your Spirit leads to an abundant life full of peace, joy, and happiness. I choose Your Spirit today. Continue to help me bring my flesh in line with Your Will. In Jesus name, Amen and Amen!!!!

Day 352: Expect Good. Why? Because God Is Good!

I have a question for you: What are you hoping for? What are you expecting in life? Are you looking for something good to happen, or are you expecting to be disappointed?

No matter what you may be going through right now in your life, God is good. Just continue to put your trust in Him, and you will be victorious. Jesus did not die for us to be saddened, depressed, and hopeless. He died so that we could be full of hope and have life more abundantly.

The devil wants to steal your joy and hope, and he will lie to you. Don't let him. The devil might say your situation will never get better. He'll say God won't heal you, that's why you are still battling health challenges. He also might tell you nothing good can happen in your life, or that the things you care about won't last. Don't ever listen to that Devil. Begin to listen and speak what God's Word says.

Remember, our God is good, and He has good plans for your life as well as my life. If you will maintain your hope, continue to trust and believe, especially in the midst of troubled and uncertain times, He has promised you "double for your trouble." So, refuse to give up hope. Start expecting God to do something—something good! In Jesus name, Amen!! Amen!!!

Let us pray:

Lord, my hope is in You. Satan is a liar, and I will not listen to him and lose hope. I expect You to do good things in my life because you are a good God. I will continue to trust and believe in your Word. You are God that will never leave me nor forsake me. You are a God that will supply all my needs according to your riches and glory by Christ Jesus. You are Everything I will ever need. I just want to say thank you Lord. In Jesus name, Amen and Amen!!!!!

Day 353: Take Hold Of Your Blessings

Scriptures says:

For we are God's masterpiece. He has created us anew in Christ Jesus, so we can do the good things He planned for us long ago.

Ephesians 2:10 NLT

My brothers and sisters, God wants to lead us into the promises He has for us. Once we have been recreated in Christ, born anew, we can experience the good life that God prearranged for us, which is to enjoy the blessings and be a blessing. But to follow God into that life, we must BELIEVE His Word and that means some things will need to change in our life.

Now, don't be afraid of the word *change;* it just means that we need to stop doing some things we've been doing and start doing some things we haven't been doing. Amen! For example, PLEASE stop thinking negative thoughts and start thinking POSITIVELY, stop settling in your comfort zone and step out of the boat, stop procrastinating and start taking the opportunities that arise. Also, we must stop putting ourselves first and we must put God's Word First.

It's not enough to just read about and talk about the blessings. We must decide that we are going to take hold of our blessings that God has provided for us. God is good; We must be willing to follow and accept the positive changes that God wants to bring to our life as He prepares us to enjoy the blessings and to be a blessing to others.

My brothers and sisters, I encourage you to make the necessary changes to get in agreement with God's Word. You know what you've been doing and what you haven't been doing. Keep it real with yourself!!! Let's experience God's blessings!!!! In Jesus name, Amen!!!

Let us pray:

Holy Spirit, show me the changes I need to make in order to possess all that you have provided for me. Thank You for preparing me to be a blessing to others and fulfill the destiny You have for my life. In Jesus name, Amen!!!!

Day 354: Forget The Past, Move Forward

My brothers and sisters, it will be an exceptionally long journey to freedom, peace and joy if we never let our past go. We will never be able to move forward and experience all that God has for us if we continue to relive our past. Forget about the past and move forward. In Jesus name, Amen!!!

Scriptures says:

No, dear brothers and sisters, I have not achieved it, but I focus on this one thing: Forgetting the past and looking forward to what lies ahead.

Philippians 3:13 NLT

Day 355: Pray And Wait

See, we have bad habits of trying to fix our situations, problems, circumstances, and people the way we want it to be. Wrong method!

For example, let's say you are married, or trying to change a loved one, or you have issues with a co-worker. Stop trying to make him/her be what you want them to be. Instead, Pray and talk to the Lord. He can fix the situation better than you can, but you have to truly trust Him. A lot of times when we try to fix it our way and we don't get immediate results, then tension forms, negative thoughts and feelings arise, and fear begins to develop.

Here's the problem: you then become frustrated, irritated, angry, and stressed when trying to force a situation yourself instead of praying and waiting while God works on your behalf. The Bible tells us in 1 Peter 5:7 NLT: "Give all your worries and cares to God, for He cares about you." When you do this, the Lord is working it out.

So stop trying to fix a person or change the situation how you want it to be. Give it God, pray, and wait, and watch the results. In Jesus name, Amen and Amen!!!

Day 356: We Must Stay Connected To God

Scriptures says:

Yes, I am the vine; you are the branches. Those who remain in me, and I in them, will produce much fruit. For apart from me you can do nothing.

John 15:5 NLT

Think about this Scripture for a second: Basically, if we are apart from God or if we are not connected to God, then we shall struggle in whatever circumstances and situations that we may face.

Imagine a fresh garden in your backyard with all kinds of fresh, ripe and tasty fruits, vegetables, and grapevines. See, God desires that our lives be like those fresh fruits, veggies and grapevines. However, the only way to experience fruitfulness is to stay connected with God. If we do this, then it allows God to cultivate, weed and prune us. First, to get rid of that negative mindset. Secondly, to grow spiritually. Thirdly, to agree with His Word so that we can experience all that He has for our lives.

My brothers and sisters, let's continue to remain connected to God so that we can experience Peace, Comfort, Strength, Joy, Happiness, and Healing. In Jesus name, Amen!!!

But if you remain in me and my words remain in you, you may ask for anything you want, and it will be granted!

John 15:7 NLT

Day 357: Weapons For Victory

Okay, listen...

Scriptures says:

Dear brothers and sisters, when troubles of any kind come your way, consider it an opportunity for great joy.

James 1:2 NLT

This Scripture tells us that we will have trials and tribulations, but we should consider it an opportunity for great joy. In order for us to do this, we need the mighty help of the Lord to continue to fight off Satan in order to experience joy.

Here's what we must do: First, we must get in God's Word: Receive it through preaching, teaching, reading, and private Bible study. Secondly, we must Praise Him: This defeats the devil faster and more efficiently than any other battle plan, but it must be genuine heart-praise, not just lip-service or a religious ritual. Thirdly, we must exercise Prayer: Prayer is communication with God, asking Him for help or talking with Him about whatever is on your heart. To have an effective prayer life, we must develop an intimate, personal relationship with the Father. Fourthly, we must confess the Word of God. We must speak His Word. We must call things that be not as though they were. Finally, we must Believe!!!!!!!

My brothers and sisters, I genuinely believe that if we apply these biblical weapons then we will experience all that God has for us. In Jesus name, Amen!!

Let us pray:

Lord, thank You so much for giving me the spiritual weapons I need to fight the enemy, overcome burdens, and receive my manifestation. With Your help, I know that I can win the battle today because Victory is mine. I claim it, I believe it and I receive it right now in Jesus name, Amen and Amen!!!!!!

Day 358: Be A True Worshipper

Let me explain:

Worship is so, so, so much more than just singing songs. It is a condition of the heart and a state of mind. We can worship God passionately without even singing a single note. Our worship for God is in our hearts, it fills our thoughts, and it is expressed through our mouths and through our bodies.

The world often thinks of worship as "religion," which is not the case. True worshipping is about a personal relationship, spiritual intimacy, and passionate expressions of devotion from people who love God with all their hearts. This is true worship.

The Bible says that God is seeking those who worship Him "in spirit and in truth."

I find it interesting that He does not want just anybody to worship Him. He wants true and genuine people. He does not want to be worshiped out of fear, obligation, or religion.

True worship is a result of intimacy with God. Worship God today with your whole heart and be a worshiper in spirit and in truth!

Let us Pray:

Lord, I don't just want to offer You lip service. Instead, I give my life to You as a true worshiper, intimately connected with You. You are so good to me and I want to worship You "in spirit and in truth." In Jesus name, Amen!!!

Day 359: With God, All Things Are Possible

Scriptures says:

Jesus looked at them intently and said, "Humanly speaking, it is impossible. But with God everything is possible."

Matthew 19:26 NLT

Ok: Think about this Scripture for a second. Clear as day it says all things are possible with God. Not SOME things but ALL things are possible. Basically, no matter what you may be believing God for, it will come to pass as long as you agree with God's Word.

Ok: Now, this means God has to be first and in the center of everything. Bible tells us in Matthew 6:33 NLT, "Seek the Kingdom of God above all else, and live righteously, and He will give you everything you need."

Ok: We just read two Scriptures basically stating that if we put God first, get in agreement with His Word and Believe His Word then All things and Everything is possible and shall be provided.

See, the issue with Believing is the real problem of why we don't see manifestation in our situations. Whatever issues we have right now today has already been worked out. Do you believe this??? See, you trying to figure out HOW God gonna do it and WHEN He gonna do it. Truth of the matter: it's already done. Our job is to Believe it's done by Trusting God's Word. Then we begin to experience rest and peace. Once we get to this point, then we will see a SHIFT in our situations. "With God, All Things Are Possible." In Jesus name, Amen!!!!! Amen!!!

Day 360: Blessings Upon Everyone!

Let us pray:

Dear Lord, We come before you to give you thanks. This is the day that you have made, and we rejoice and be glad unto it today and every day. We thank you for a heart free of sadness. Lord We thank you for a mind free of worries. Lord We thank you for a life full of gladness. Lord We thank you for a body free of illness. Lord We thank for restored marriages. Lord We thank you that nothing is missing, nothing is lacking, and nothing is broken in our lives. Lord you've been so good to us. We just thank you. In Jesus name, Amen and Amen!!!!!!

Day 361: Get Rid Of Unrealistic Expectations

Unrealistic expectations can quickly steal our peace and joy. Why? Because we usually visualize a perfect day, with perfect people, and ourselves being perfectly happy in our perfect little world, but we all know that isn't reality. The Bible tells us in John 16:33 NLT, "I have told you all this so that you may have peace in me. Here on earth, you will have many trials and sorrows. But take heart because I have overcome the world."

This Scripture tells us plain as day that we will experience some sort of troubles along our journey. We need to be prepared when troubles do come. There is no perfect life. In reality, only God is perfect, and the rest of us are under construction.

The devil knows what steals our peace, and he sets us up to get upset when our unrealistic expectations fall apart. We must develop a new mindset and get in agreement with God's Word.

All of us has to deal with inconveniences, but we can deal with them with a positive attitude and avoid a bad attitude. Remember today that only God is perfect, and trust in Him. He can always lead you past disappointing circumstances, strengthening you and helping you to hold onto your peace.

Let us pray:

God, only You are perfect. I am so glad that even when people and circumstances fail, You never do. Instead of putting my hope in things that will disappoint, I choose a life of peace that only comes from putting my hope in You. In Jesus name, Amen and Amen!!!!

Day 362: Living For God Is All That Matters

I can tell you right now, it takes boldness to follow God instead of the crowd. Being excessively concerned about what others think leads only to confusion, being stressed, and depressed. Although all of us enjoy being well-thought of, however, it's not possible to be liked by everyone all the time. Don't worry about trying to compare your life with someone else. God has for you what He has for you. Live according to the Word.

Folks who are real friends will help you be all God wants you to be. They won't judge you for following God's call. Real friends will encourage you to make God number one in your life and maybe they will look to you for advice, wisdom and Godly counsel which gives God great Joy.

Even if everyone else walks away from you, He promises to never leave you or forsake you.

Life gets too complicated, confusing and frustrating when we try to please both God and people. You don't have to compare yourself to anyone and worry what people think about you. Live life for God and be free to be who He made you to be. Amen!

Let us pray:

Lord, I decide right now live for You alone. Living by other people's standards and expectations for me will get me nowhere. You are the only One who matters, and I will be the person You've made me to be. In Jesus name, Amen and Amen!!!!

Day 363: Do Not Give In To Defeat

If we live defeated lives, then we simply are not trusting God, and seem to have given up on His Word. Victory won't appear with this type of mentality. Thinking only about oneself, feeling loss and defeat, only blinds us to our blessings and the possibilities before us, and it steals our hope for both today and tomorrow.

Please!! Be encouraged, my Brothers and Sisters, that you do not waste one more day of your life in defeat. When you lose hope and begin to feel sorry for yourself, STOP and SAY: "I refuse to feel sorry for myself. I may be in a difficult season of life right now, but I will not stop hoping for better things and I will put my trust in God's Word!"

God has thoughts and plans for your good, to give you hope for your future. If you will hold onto your hope, and fight for it when the enemy tries to take it away, you will see amazing things take place in your life. Amen!!

Let us pray:

God, I refuse to feel sorry for myself. I shall not be deterred or defeated. Even if things are difficult right now, I know that You are bigger than my problems and that You have a good future planned for me. I want Your plans to come to pass in my life, and I trust in You to change my circumstances according to Your will. In Jesus name, Amen and Amen!!

Day 364: Whatever You've Been Believing God For, He Has Already Worked It Out

Let me explain:

Whatever you've been praying to God about, He has already worked it out. Your job is to continue to truly Believe what God's Word says. There is no need to allow yourself to be stressed and depressed over a temporary situation. Remember that we serve a God that can do far beyond what we think or imagine. Just calm down! It hurts now, but just wait for Him. He will prove to be faithful.

The Lord and His grace are everlasting. God is moving in ways you don't understand right now. Be still and allow Him to calm the storm in your heart.

Believe that God is going to come through no matter how the situation looks, or how long it appears to be taking. Continue to Believe God's Word, and stay in Faith. My brothers and sisters, the Lord has worked it out. In Jesus name, Amen and Amen!!!

Scriptures says:

Don't let your hearts be troubled. Trust in God, and trust also in me.

John 14:1 NLT

Day 365: Hold On, It's Coming In Due Season

Let me explain:

Due season is important. Due season is the season that you will reap what you harvest. However, we don't know when due season will come. Just continue to do well. God will Bless.

See, people mess up in due season, people quit in due season, people treat others wrong in due season, people walk out on you in due season, sometimes we get tired in due season. The devil just want us to quit in our due season. Due season is a period of testing. Due season is a period of trial. WHAT WILL YOU DO DURING THE DUE SEASON?????

Let me tell you: All we need to do is continue to stay in faith and stay in agreement with God's Word. I'm here to let you know, my Brothers and Sisters, that you will get through it. Continue to BELIEVE that you are close to what God has for you. Your due season is right around the corner. In Jesus name, Amen and Amen!!!

Scriptures says:

And let us not be weary in well doing for in due season we shall reap, if we faint not.

Galatians 6:9 KJV

About the Author

Marlon and Shanae Brown are parents of two lovely daughters, and are located in Orlando, Florida. In 2019, God put a vision in their hearts that they chose to pursue and honor. They began Promise Principles (www.promiseprinciples.com), a small business that creates amazing designs meant to bless and inspire others through positive reminders of God's principles for T-shirts.

You can contact Marlon at:

info@promiseprinciples.com

Milton Keynes UK
Ingram Content Group UK Ltd.
UKHW020621071223
433828UK00015B/747